CHICKEN SOUP FOR THE WOMAN GOLFER'S SOUL

CHICKEN SOUP FOR THE WOMAN GOLFER'S SOUL

Stories About Trailblazing Women Who've Changed the Game Forever

Jack Canfield
Mark Victor Hansen
Matthew E. Adams
Patty Aubery

Health Communications, Inc.
Deerfield Beach, Florida

www.hcibooks.com
www.chickensoup.com

We would like to acknowledge the many publishers and individuals who granted us permission to reprint the cited material. (Note: The stories that were penned anonymously or were written by Jack Canfield, Mark Victor Hansen, Matthew E. Adams, and Patty Aubery are not included in this listing.)

No Guys on This Trip Please. Reprinted by permission of Katharine Dyson. ©2005 Katharine Dyson.

Drive Dynamics. Reprinted by permission of Marilynn Smith. ©2006 Marilynn Smith.

My First "Lady's Day" Golf Outing. Reprinted by permission of Betty King. ©2006 Betty King.

Out of the Rough. Reprinted by permission of Kathryn A. Beisner. ©2006 Kathryn A. Beisner.

The 150-Yard Memorial. Reprinted by permission of Nancy L. Lewis. ©2006 Nancy L. Lewis.

(Continued on page 252)

Library of Congress Cataloging-in-Publication Data

Chicken soup for the woman golfer's soul : stories about trailblazing women who've changed the game forever / Jack Canfield . . . [et al.].

   p. cm.

   ISBN-13: 978-0-7573-0580-1

   ISBN-10: 0-7573-0580-6

   1. Women golfers—United States—Anecdotes. 2. Golfers—Anecdotes. 3. Golf—Anecdotes. I. Canfield, Jack, 1944-

   GV966.C49 2007

   796.352082—dc22

                                     2006037035

Publisher: Health Communications, Inc.
          3201 S.W. 15th Street
          Deerfield Beach, FL 33442-8190

Cover photo of Michelle Wie: © Rob Tringali/SportsChrome
Cover photo of Nancy Lopez: © Tony Tomsic/SportsChrome
Cover photo of Lorena Ochoa: © Lisa Blumenfeld/Getty Images
Cover photo of Annika Sorenstam: © Scott Halleran/Getty Images
Cover design by Larissa Hise Henoch
Inside formatting by Dawn Von Strolley Grove

This book is dedicated to the female visionaries and pioneers who have helped to make golf a game that can be enjoyed by all people in equal measure.

Contents

3. A Game for All Generations

4. Golf Is a Beautiful Walk

5. Unforgettable Moments

6. Joy and Sorrow

7. Tomorrow's Tee Time

Acknowledgments

We wish to express our heartfelt gratitude to the following people who helped make this book possible:

Our families, who have been chicken soup for our souls!

Jack's family, Inga, Travis, Riley, Christopher, Oran, and Kyle for all their love and support.

Mark's family, Patty, Elisabeth, and Melanie Hansen, for once again sharing and lovingly supporting us in creating yet another book.

Matthew's wife, Donna Adams, and his two sons, Austin and CJ, for their patience while their dad worked on another book.

Thank you to Patty's husband, Jeff Aubery, and her two wonderful sons, JT and Chandler.

While nothing comes without a cost, it is our families who make the greatest sacrifice in allowing us countless hours to work on our books. That is time that really belongs to them.

Thank you also to Laura Neal of the Ladies Professional Golf Association (LPGA) and all of the LPGA golfers who shared their wonderful stories with us. We are humbled by your accomplishments.

Our publisher Peter Vegso, for his vision and commitment to bringing *Chicken Soup for the Soul* to the world.

Russ Kalmaski, for being there on every step of the journey, with love, laughter, and endless creativity.

Barbara LoMonaco, for nourishing us with truly wonderful stories and cartoons.

D'ette Corona, for being there to answer any questions along the way.

Patty Hansen, for her thorough and competent handling of the legal and licensing aspects of the Chicken Soup for the Soul books. You are magnificent at the challenge!

Veronica Romero, Teresa Esparza, Robin Yerian, Jesse Ianniello, Lauren Edelstein, Laurie Hartman, Patti Clement, Maegan Romanello, Noelle Champagne, Jody Emme, Debbie Lefever, Michelle Adams, Dee Dee Romanello, Shanna Vieyra, and Gina Romanello, who support Jack's and Mark's businesses with skill and love.

We wish to make a special acknowledgment and express a deep respect and appreciation for the writing skills of Carol McAdoo Rehme, who worked tirelessly with many of our celebrity contributors to ensure their words and messages will inspire millions for generations to come. Carol, we are awed by your many talents and are indebted to you for your contributions. This book simply would not exist without your considerable input.

Michele Matrisciani, Andrea Gold, Allison Janse, Katheline St. Fort, and Carol Rosenberg, our editors at Health Communications, Inc., for their devotion to excellence.

Terry Burke, Lori Golden, Kelly Maragni, Sean Geary, Patricia McConnell, Ariana Falerni, Kim Weiss, and Paola Fernandez-Rana, the sales, marketing, and PR departments at Health Communications, Inc., for doing such an incredible job supporting our books.

Tom Sand, Claude Choquette, and Luc Jutras, who manage year after year to get our books translated into thirty-six languages around the world.

The art department at Health Communications, Inc., for their talent, creativity, and unrelenting patience in producing book covers and inside designs that capture the essence of Chicken Soup: Larissa Hise Henoch, Lawna Patterson Oldfield, Andrea Perrine Brower, Anthony Clausi, and Dawn Von Strolley Grove.

All the Chicken Soup for the Soul coauthors, who make it so much of a joy to be part of this Chicken Soup family.

Our glorious panel of readers who helped us make the final selections and provided invaluable suggestions on how to improve the book.

And, most of all, everyone who submitted their heartfelt stories, poems, quotes, and cartoons for possible inclusion in this book. While we were not able to use everything you sent in, we know that each word came from a magical place flourishing within your soul.

Because of the size of this project, we may have left out the names of some people who contributed along the way. If so, we are sorry, but please know that we really do appreciate you very much.

We are truly grateful and love you all!

Introduction

Golf has always been a game requiring great skill, where agility and intelligence go hand in hand and patience is more than a virtue. Discipline, dedication, determination, humility, tranquillity, companionship, competition, physical and mental exercise, and so much more are all qualities that comprise the great game of golf. It is a sport that transcends the mere confines of the manicured field upon which it is played. To be a golfer is to embrace a sport that seems to permeate every aspect of your life. It is about more than simply being a fan; it is a lifestyle choice and a lifelong journey.

For those who love the game, their long journey begins with an infatuation, develops into a senseless love, and matures into the kind of contentious, maddening, frustrating, exhilarating, fulfilling, and yet understanding kind of bond you see in an elderly couple in the park.

Women have been a part of the game of golf since its earliest days. From Mary, Queen of Scots, to today's current crop of young, exciting athletes, the game has come a long way since the days of flowing Victorian-era dresses and hickory-shafted golf clubs.

In the early 1900s, amateur golfers dominated the game of golf, and the female golfers from the British Isles, such as Joyce Wethered, ruled the day. But by the third decade of the century, the United States started to produce female golfing stars who would define the game for the next twenty-five years. These included Patty Berg, Babe Didrikson Zaharias, and Betty Jameson.

In the postwar years, the country saw explosive growth in both economic means and the game of golf. Women have not always been recognized in the sport the same way men have, though. It wasn't until the middle of the twentieth century that women were allowed to play professionally, and for years many golf courses forbade women to play—and some still do. But women golfers over the past several decades have used their tenacity, skill, and intellect to overcome these obstacles and are now not only recognized in the sport, but they are changing it. By 1950, the Ladies Professional Golf Association (LPGA) was established, paving the way for female athletes to compete for purses that today number in the millions of dollars and provides a stage for superstars like Annika Sörenstam, Karrie Webb, Laura Davies, Lorena Ochoa, Se Ri Pak, Paula Creamer, Christine Kerr, and Natalie Gulbis, among others.

It is an exciting time for the game of golf, and women's golf in particular. We decided to write this book to celebrate the game's noble past, its dynamic present, and its exciting future. The story of women's golf is a story of vision, determination, overcoming obstacles and adversity, and the pure enjoyment of a game that teaches as much about life as it does about birdies, pars, and bogies. As golf is a reflection of life, we are confident this book will equally appeal to our nongolfing readers as the universal stories of hope, charity, love, support, and perspective are in keeping with the rich heritage of Chicken Soup for the Soul stories you have come to know.

We hope that you enjoy this tour through the world of women's golf with as much joy, amazement, and respect as we have had putting this book together.

Share with Us

We would love to hear your reactions to the stories in this book. Please let us know what your favorite stories were and how they affected you.

We also invite you to send us stories you would like to see published in future editions of *Chicken Soup for the Soul*. Please send submissions to: www.chickensoup.com.

Chicken Soup for the Soul
P.O. Box 30880
Santa Barbara, CA 93130
fax: 805-563-2945

We hope you enjoy reading this book as much as we enjoyed compiling, editing, and writing it.

1

IT'S OUR TIME

Theme: The Changing Face
of Women's Golf

*I go into the locker room and find a corner
and just sit there. I try to achieve a peaceful
state of nothingness that will carry over onto
the golf course. If I can get that feeling of
quiet and obliviousness within myself, I feel I
can't lose.*

Jane Blalock

No Guys on This Trip Please

Friends are people who help you be more your-self, more the person you are intended to be.

Merle Shain

When Allison invited us to her winter pad for a long week-end of golf, my first reaction was, "Are you crazy! Just a bunch of girls? No guys? No hand-holding strolls on a moonlit beach? No dancing under the stars?" I could not imagine it. To me, a tropical getaway spelled romance. Love stuff.

But not wanting to be left out of something that, who knows, might actually turn out to be a good thing, I couldn't say no. And let's face it, these were my friends, my lunch group, my weekly Thursday foursome. I knew I could be replaced, and there was no way I wanted to be left out and then have to hear them go on and on about their next outing.

I didn't want to listen to them rehashing the great golf, dinners at the club, and the fantastic off-season bargains in the pro shop, that cute yellow golf shirt that was half price. I wanted to be part of it. To belong. So I packed a bag and, dragging my clubs in my black canvas travel bag with the tiny little wheels, headed to the airport with the girls.

And you guessed it. We had a great time. Played golf at three different courses, three days in a row; ate fried clams and calamari at a local fish place; laughed ourselves silly over stupid things, our unbridled giddiness no doubt nudged along by pitchers of margaritas; and stayed up late into the night playing vicious, competitive games of Taboo.

We took a couple of lessons at one of the clubs and actually got out to the courses early so we could practice. We played skins for ten cents a hole and bet a dollar on closest to the hole on the par threes. We were relaxed. Happy.

The next year, we couldn't wait to make a date to do it all over again. But we made a major mistake. We talked too much. Our men heard us wax poetic over the condition of the golf courses, the clubby bars. Oh, we were so smug. We even mentioned, barely mentioned, the hot lady pro at one of the clubs. Super swing she had. Great clothes.

"Hey, sounds like a good time," said Allison's husband as we all sat having dinner one night.

"Yeah," said Jimmy. "What do you say we join you on the next trip? We'll have a ball."

"Ah, humm," we all said quietly, thinking.

"Good idea," I said. "But what about your annual Myrtle Beach outing with the guys?"

"What about it?" said Jimmy.

"Isn't it the last weekend in April?"

"That's the date."

"Well, that's a shame," said Allison (she was always a quick study). "That's the same weekend we're going on our trip."

"That's right. Pity you won't be able to join us," I added, wearing my best sad face while making a mental note to add our girlie golf trip to my calendar now that we had a firm date. Oh yeah.

Katharine Dyson

Drive Dynamics

Life shrinks or expands in proportion to one's courage.

Anaïs Nin

We were golfers.

We were dreamers.

We were pioneers.

In 1950, thirteen of us cofounded the Ladies Professional Golf Association (LPGA). I was an enthusiastic twenty-one. The youngest, Marlene Bauer, was an energetic sixteen; the oldest, Babe Zaharias, was an athletic thirty-eight. And we each set out to prove that women could earn a living as touring golf professionals.

During those early years, we placed our faith *and* our money in the LPGA. All of us tithed 10 percent of our meager winnings into the treasury to supplement funds and keep the organization solvent. We served as our own staff and handled administrative duties: public relations, scouting new tournaments, and writing prize-money checks.

In order to gain a foothold in this male-dominated game, we had to sell ourselves—as well as our tour—and worked hard to promote our tournaments and grow our galleries. We held press conferences, spoke at civic luncheons, and made radio and television appearances. *Sports Illustrated* even featured us in style shows at the Dallas Civitan and the LPGA Championship in Las Vegas. Decked out in heels and hats, dresses and gloves, we hit the runways to prove that women could be both athletic and feminine. (I always wore a skirt and pearls on the course.)

But our biggest challenge—and best memory maker— was life on the road. It was a far cry from today's tour travel and prize purses. Few of us could afford airfare, so we crisscrossed the country in a string of cars, driving caravan-style. Riding two to a vehicle, we were loaded. Golf bags, shoes, clothes, cosmetics. Everything we needed.

Jackie Pung even brought her two daughters. A few brought their dogs. And Wiffi Smith brought her piano. It nearly filled her motor home, but she viewed it as a necessity: She said it was her favorite training device for strengthening her fingers.

Like a big family, we wiled away the miles, the hours, the days. We sang and we laughed and we squabbled. When we needed to stop, we held cardboard paddles out the window. One indicated food, another gas, and a third meant potty time. When a car broke down—which happened all too frequently—every car stopped. Blowouts were common, and we helped each other change the tires. When we needed counseling or consoling, we helped each other then, too. Someone was always ready with the wisdom and the words.

On the course we were competitors, but on the road we were comrades. Sisters.

Once we hit town, we set to work like the team we were. Our top priorities included a Laundromat, a hairdresser, and a desperately needed practice round. We attended sponsor parties. We met our press commitments. We handled the course setup, pin placements, and pairings ourselves.

And *then* we played golf. From the men's tees. Our courses measured a staggering 6,250 to 6,950 yards, yet we posted some remarkable scores under some amazing conditions.

Even more remarkable, over the next decade we kindled a flame of interest in women's golf and helped bring it to the forefront of American sports. It took vision and grit and teamwork. It took all of us—plus many others who caught our vision and drive. But we did it.

Because we were golfers.

Because we were dreamers.

Because we were . . . friends.

Marilynn Smith

My First "Lady's Day" Golf Outing

I will never forget my first "lady's day" golf outing!

Barbara and I were next-door neighbors with children around the same age; need I say more? We were always looking for something to define ourselves, something besides being just "mothers." We were also concerned with keeping our girlish figures. We were walking partners, but the path we took was becoming old hat; we needed some new scenery.

I noticed an advertisement for lady's golf lessons in our local newspaper, just as warmer weather and its sunshine began to descend on the Midwest.

I loved the sun; spring and summer were my favorite times of the year. Anything I could do to help absorb the sun and give me more exercise was tops on my list. But golfing was something my husband was good at; me—that was another story!

The advertisement for golfing lessons jumped out at me. Perhaps if I took a few lessons I could at least learn how to hit that little white ball off the tee. Maybe I could get good enough to spend time on the course with my husband, perhaps even join other couples in a round of golf.

"Barbara, do you know how to golf?" I asked.

"No," she answered.

"Would you be interested in learning?" I inquired.

That is the conversation that led up to our golf lessons and our first "lady's day" golf outing of the season.

During our lessons we learned the proper stance, swing, and where the fairway and greens were. We also learned where the rough was and that we were not supposed to aim in that direction! We finally learned, occasionally, to hit one of the tiny little white golf balls off the tee. BUT we also learned that when you join the "lady's day" summer league, you have to count every time you swing at the ball in totaling up your score!

I'll never forget the day I discovered that golf balls come in colors besides the generic shade of white. Wow! Blue, pink, and yellow golf balls; I loved the game already!

Our lessons barely behind us, Barbara and I went out for a day of golf. With the rule to count every stroke ingrained in our brains, and being the honest women we were, we took our scorecards along to record every swing.

Because we were taking up golfing as much for exercise as for the sunshine, we opted to pull our golf bags instead of using the golf carts—big mistake!

Now, do you know how many times two inexperienced women can swing a golf club during one round of golf on a nine-hole golf course? Don't ask! Let's just put it this way—when we finished up the last hole and the moon was looming over the horizon, making it nearly impossible to find even a shocking pink golf ball on the green, much less in the rough, my husband was at the clubhouse preparing for an all-out search party!

Barbara and I went on to improve slightly, get lots of sun and exercise, and enjoy the company of other ladies on "lady's day" throughout the summer season. I also joined my husband on the course for several years, until multiple sclerosis took away my ability to walk. It didn't take away my memory, though, or my ability to laugh, as I often do when I remember that first "lady's day" after-dark golf outing!

Betty King

"I shot my age on that hole!"

Out of the Rough

*Don't fear the space between your dreams and
reality. If you can dream it, you can do it.*

Belva Davis

Mom was a newlywed when she first played golf in
1943. Friends invited her and Dad to play a round of eighteen holes. Mom went out to the golf course without hesi-
tation or the first inkling about the game that would
become her lifeline.

Mom's passionate pursuit of the game was set in
motion when Sergeant Haskell, the golf instructor at
Barksdale Air Force Base, told her, "You'll never be a good
golfer because you're just too big at the top." His opinion
of her stance was that she couldn't reach the ball because
of her generous bosom.

Lesson #1: Don't ever tell my mom she can't do something. In response to Sergeant Haskell's prediction, Mom
has filled her golf bag, wardrobe, jewelry box, and étagère
with prizes she has won on the golf course.

Mom is a natural athlete, and she's competitive. In the
1950s, golf was considered an acceptable sport for women.

Golf did not require women to run, bump into each other, or perspire too much. And golf was defined by a strict set of rules, which made it perfect for an officer's wife.

Using the handicap system designed for amateur golfers, Mom was able to play with the best of them. She joined the ladies' golf club at each new billet, and her teammates marveled at her ability to win.

Lesson #2: Don't ever challenge my mom to a golf match. That's because she's hard to beat when there is loot involved. Her golf buddies once said, "All you need to do is put a nickel in front of Judy and watch her go!" She brims with confidence every time she repeats this story.

None of us can imagine how Mom would have dealt with life's disappointments without golf. It provided the right amount of distance between her and the anguish of parenthood caused by five kids.

In fact, golf saved Mom's life when I was born. She gave birth to me in a military Quonset hut in the suffocating heat of Kansas in August. Back at home with two youngsters and a baby, she shut the car door on my two-year-old sister's finger. In shock, Carolyn wailed, "Mommy, you hurt me!" That moment, on top of the postpartum adjustments every mother endures, sent her over the edge. She began to doubt her mothering skills, afraid she might hurt one of us again.

Aunt Mary took the train from Pennsylvania to Kansas to take care of us three girls while Mom got her confidence back.

With Aunt Mary shouldering the burden of child care, Mom was able to get things in perspective. Accidents were bound to happen. But with all of her focus on child rearing, the slightest mishap had seemed like a personal failure. Mom needed something for herself, something where she could control the outcome and nobody got hurt. Mom needed golf.

In golf, Mom found the perfect diversion. It was every-thing that mothering wasn't. Golf was quiet, composed, and precise. Mothering was noisy, confused, and ambiguous. Golf was clean and orderly. Mothering was messy and chaotic. Golf was played with grown-ups, and mothering was all about kids.

But golf was also expressive. Behind the veneer of polite courtesy was an unspoken tolerance for a full range of human emotions that were unacceptable in all other aspects of military life. Men could hook the ball off the tee and use colorful language in mixed company. Women could smirk and say, "Well, I guess the honors are mine, again," while their opponents seethed. It was the sort of release Mom needed.

It was golf that carried her through the last, tumultuous years of my dad's life as he struggled with Alzheimer's disease. When he began to ask who she was, and he couldn't remember that he had just finished eating breakfast, Mom knew that he couldn't be left at home alone. But the alternatives were unbearable. Mom had promised Dad she wouldn't put him in a nursing home.

I stayed with Dad while Mom played golf on ladies' day. Soon it was clear that five hours a week was not enough to replenish the strength needed for her twenty-four-hour caregiving duties. It was excruciating for Mom to decide to take Dad to a drop-in senior care facility while she took more frequent breaks to maintain her sanity.

Dad died at home three years later. In the church annex, after the funeral service, a woman introduced herself to me as knowing Mom from the golf club. I recognized her name and thanked her for being a friend to Mom these last years. She said, "Oh, she'll be all right. She's a tough bird."

Indeed, Mom has been all right. She has regained the youthful exuberance of so many decades ago. She often plays golf with women my age, who remark afterward,

"When I grow up, I want to be just like you, Judy!"

At the golf course, she has deepened her friendships with women who have experienced similar end-of-life issues with their spouses. These relationships are so important to her that she cautions us not to take her away from her friends when she gets to the point of needing care. In fact, her wish for her own demise is to drop dead on the eighteenth green . . . after she putts out to win the match, of course.

Lesson #3: Don't ever underestimate the power of golf.

Kathryn Beisner

"Who's gonna stay here and do my homework?"

The 150-Yard Memorial

It was a warm summer afternoon at Maple River Country Club. The last day of the beginning women's golf clinic was about to start; seven women would soon be graduating into the scary world of country club golf. The last lesson consisted of playing the first hole in a scramble format while reviewing the protocol, vernacular, and gamesmanship of the sport.

As we ventured down the fairway together, all were beginning to enjoy their experience while their nerves began to settle. As we strolled along, four of the ladies were talking about how they were going to join the "nine-holers" as soon as possible. I noticed that the other three were heading over to the 150-yard marker. Alice Brown, one of the ladies congregated around the marker, waived me over and asked, "Who passed away?" I wasn't sure why she asked the question, nor was I aware of any member who had recently died. I asked Mrs. Brown why she asked and she replied, "This is a very nice memorial, and we were just curious who it was in memory of because we haven't noticed any plaque."

The 150-yard markers at Maple River Country Club consisted of a boulder, some ornamental grasses, flowers, and a small tree. Realizing that she and the others who were paying homage mistakenly thought this 150-yard marker was a memorial, I called the remainder of the class over to offer some clarity. I explained that most golf courses have some type of yardage marker on each hole and from that point to the middle of the green was 150 yards. As they looked on with puzzled faces, I further explained that these markers could be anything from a simple pole to a beautiful gardenlike display similar to the one they were surrounding.

After a few moments of awkward silence, the group all broke into laughter and were relieved that none of their fellow members had recently passed on. Mrs. Brown then brought up an interesting perspective. "Why have a marker from 150 yards away when none of us hit the ball even close to that distance on our best shot?" Good point, Mrs. Brown, good point.

Nancy Lewis

Pitching the Game

What other people may find in poetry or art museums, I find in the flight of a good drive.

Arnold Palmer

As a little girl, I had big dreams. I wanted to grow up to play professional baseball. I even had the team picked out: the St. Louis Cardinals. And I hoped to pitch for them someday.

My family always listened to Cardinal games on the radio. We were avid fans. During my adolescent years in the 1940s, I began to realize my dream on a smaller scale by pitching, managing, and coaching a boys' baseball team in my hometown of Wichita, Kansas.

After pitching one particular game, I stomped into the house. I imagine my blond pigtails slapped my back and my freckles stood out in stark relief against my flushed face.

"How did you do today, dear?" my mother asked in her sweet voice.

I threw my leather mitt against the wall and spit out, "Sh—!" . . . a word I'd picked up from the boys on my team.

Shocked, she marched me directly into the lavatory, grabbed a bar of Lifebuoy, and washed my mouth out with the harsh soap. When Dad got home from work, she told him what I'd said.

"Well," he reflected, "I believe Marilynn needs to play a more ladylike sport."

Dad promptly drove me to the Wichita Country Club and enrolled me in Saturday golf—with a class of all boys. *What a sissy game,* I thought, *hitting a little ball and chasing it.* Nevertheless, when I began to show some talent, head pro Mike Murra took me under his wing for private lessons, and it wasn't long before I was hooked on golf.

By 1949, I'd won the Kansas Women's Amateur for three consecutive years and taken the National Women's Intercollegiate title while attending the University of Kansas.

Spalding noticed my blossoming career and asked me to represent them. They would print my name on golf clubs and send me around the country to give clinics. They offered me a $5,000 salary, an unlimited expense account, and a forest green Dodge. I agreed.

But, recalling my childhood dream, I did request something in addition, and they readily complied. They tossed in two mitts and a Spalding baseball . . . so I could play catch with my caddies.

In 1950, I became one of the thirteen founding members of the Ladies Professional Golf Association (LPGA) Tour, organized in Wichita. But in those early years, some women pros spent as much time marketing the game as they did playing it. We took on speaking engagements, gave golf clinics, and modeled in clubhouse fashion shows.

I even found myself back on the baseball diamond! In Washington, D.C., Cincinnati, and—yes—St. Louis, we did exhibitions at Major League baseball games. To increase interest and garner a nice gallery, I took the microphone to introduce us—"pro-ettes" as we were called then—and offer our sales pitch: "We're members of the LPGA and we hope you all come out to watch the lady pros at our nearby tournament."

I encouraged the crowd to support women's golf with the same fervor they championed baseball. And, stepping to home plate, I used my nine iron like a pitching wedge, hitting shot after shot to center field . . . and realized a small piece of my baseball dream.

Marilynn Smith

The Name of the Game

A golf course is alive, literally. They grow, settle, and evolve. They are constantly changing. The rest of the world is also changing all the time, and it will happen whether we wish to be a part of it or not. We must embrace change to grow, learn, and advance, or we die.

Matthew E. Adams, author of *Fairways of Life*

A lot of famous people hail from Oklahoma. Neil Armstrong, Mickey Mantel, Will Rogers, Jim Thorpe, and Johnny Bench, just to name a few. But in 1959, fewer females played. In fact, I was the first woman to receive a golf scholarship to Oklahoma City University (OCU).

OCU was amazingly progressive for that era and more than willing to start a girls' golf team. But a problem arose when the university couldn't find another girl on campus who wanted to join. So I played on the men's team and ranked third among the guys.

Abe Lemmons, the coach we shared with the basketball team, was a real character. Fortunately, with him my gender was never an issue. But he understood that not everyone felt the same way.

When we drove north to Wichita for a tournament, Abe handed over our roster.

The other coach skimmed down the list. "Hmmm, S. Maxwell," he read aloud. "What does the 'S' stand for? Stan? Steve? Sam?"

Ever protective of me, Abe didn't even blink. "Sam," he pronounced with assured finality. Under his breath he added, "Sam will do."

And so it would.

His quick thinking smoothed the way, even if it did leave room for surprise each time I appeared at a new course. For the rest of my college career, I played golf under the deceptive but credulous name Abe bestowed on me—*Sam* Maxwell.

Susie Maxwell Berning

The Swing's the Thing

In the early 1980s, I developed an interest in the challenging game of golf. One of my inheritances from my divorce settlement was a set of junior boy's golf clubs that had been collecting dust in the basement. Everything else I got had a payment book with it, including a mortgage with twenty-five years left to pay.

I had been told it is pretty expensive to play golf, so I wasn't sure my budget could allow it. Hiring a babysitter only to hit balls in the woods on bad shots would be like losing dollar bills.

Neighbors and friends encouraged me to try the game. I could hear the voice of my college gym teacher during the mandatory golf lessons, "You have a natural swing." My father was an avid golfer as well. So with reliable babysitters in place and my cleaned-up set of clubs from the basement, I started to play once a week with a group of fellow teachers. We were all beginners, so it wasn't very competitive. I enjoyed the game the very first time and was totally inspired by the beautiful walk with nature, taking the time to admire the sun, the sky, the mountains, and lakes. Doing this with the companionship of three other women was remarkable and refreshing.

Of course, I did struggle with the swing and losing balls, but that was overcome by the level of enjoyment.

Golf is full of lessons when one pays attention. I feel renewed in some way each time I play. Waiting on the first tee to start the game teaches one patience, that good things are worth waiting for. It's so different from waiting in line to pay that grocery bill, which is always higher than you expected. Losing a ball in the woods teaches one how to deal with disappointment. Golfers take the five minutes allowed to look for a ball, then drop a new ball and get over it and move on. What a good principle to apply to life when you are thrown off course.

Mentally, golf provides the same level of concentration as yoga, but in an entirely different way. A round of golf is about you and your connection to yourself, the little white ball, the club, its swing, and the topography and turf of the golf course. This sport gives you an opportunity to put everything else behind you.

The game teaches us that nothing stays the same and that we have to learn to accept change in life just as readily as we do when it starts to rain or the wind starts to blow on the golf course.

Golf gives one the courage to play with better players and to take risks, resulting in one's becoming a better player and possibly a better person. The competition helps to get us out of those old, negative, comfortable ruts that have become our friends instead of our enemies.

The little white ball is a symbol of life. Sometimes it goes smoothly and in the right direction; and other times it gets off to a bad start, goes in the wrong direction, and may even get lost. But the game goes on, just like our lives. The freedom to swing the club on the tee is exhilarating because it is as if you are saying, "Look out, world, here I come!"

So after the divorce came the swing that gave me the strength to keep on swinging. This game of pleasure and companionship changed my attitude, my friendships, my energy level, and my daily outlook at spirituality both on and off the course.

Mary Murphy Fox

Reprinted by permission of Joe Kohl. ©1996 Joe Kohl.

What's Your Handicap?

Focus not on the commotion around you, but on the opportunity ahead of you.

Arnold Palmer

Golf is an inspirational game. Many of the people who play golf are inspirational to us as well. We can always mention the names of professionals like Annika Sörenstam, Paula Creamer, and Michelle Wie and stand in awe of what they can do with that little white ball.

Over the years, I've golfed with many women who inspire me. It's one sport where size doesn't matter. You can be six feet, two inches or four feet, six inches and still hit the ball equally well. Age doesn't matter either—you can be nine or ninety. Gender doesn't matter—we have professionals of both genders. Temperament doesn't matter—we've seen those who cuss and throw their clubs, and we've seen those who smile at their mistakes and go on to finish the game very well.

When I became a senior citizen, my husband and I moved into a home on the golf course in an "over fifty-five" community. This is where I discovered the true meaning of inspiration as it relates to golf. I will never forget some of the people I observed at our golf course and golf courses nearby over a fifteen-year period.

Let's take Lois, for instance (all names have been changed to protect the individual's privacy). Lois lost three-fourths of her right hand in an industrial accident. Who'd have thought she could ever play golf again! But Lois plays as good a golf game with one hand as most of us play with two. It is called fortitude.

Marianne turned eighty-six years old this year. Marianne is all of about five feet tall—just a little gal—yet she is still out there playing golf almost every day. AND she still wins some golf competitions. "I think it's the game of golf that helped me make it to this age in the first place," Marianne said. Grit!

They rushed Janice to the hospital with a blood clot in her leg. The doctors told her they might have to amputate. Long story short: they didn't have to remove her leg, but when Janice came out of the hospital, she could barely walk. She wore a brace and a lift. Her foot drooped and was difficult to control. Let's face it, she could hardly walk, let alone play golf. But within a month, Janice tried to do just that—golf! She'd drag that leg around and push it into her setup position to prepare to tee off. Within a few more months, Janice's leg began to semicooperate on its own, and she did her best to golf right along with the rest of us. Two years later, there is little sign of her trauma and she is out there winning tournaments again. Courage!

Sally Johnson likes to play golf. She always plays with her friend, Barb. If Barb can't go with her, Sally doesn't play. There must be plenty of other people for Sally to play with, you say? Well, not too many of us would take on a blind woman. I don't know which woman presented the most determination, Barb or Sally. Barb makes sure Sally lines up in the right direction and tees the ball for her.

That's all it takes. Sally is a great ball-striker! The two of them travel in the golf cart together. Barb always finds the ball for Sally and lines her up again, over and over, until they finish eighteen holes. Willpower.

One of the golfers in our group of women began to irritate a lot of her friends. At first, she annoyed us because she never showed up at the course on time, or she'd forget her golf shoes and have to drive back home to get them; it always seemed to be something. It got worse over time. You just gritted your teeth and wondered what she would forget today! Personally, Linda always brushed it off. As time wore on, and the situation worsened, I asked Linda to lunch, determined to mention it to her. She hung her head so low I felt sorry for asking. With tears in her eyes, she explained that she had been diagnosed as being in the first phases of Alzheimer's disease. "I want to play as long as I can," she pleaded. Once her friends understood, we all began to help Linda. Some agreed to pick her up and make sure she had her equipment with her. It worked for an especially long time. Linda may not have had the strength of mind, but she had the resolve.

Not much of a golfer, Anne still played because she had fun at it. Everyone enjoyed playing with Anne in spite of her high handicap. "Isn't it a great day?" she'd say. "At my age, it sure is nice to be on the top side of the grass!" Anne's spirit made you want to have her around. She always made you smile. "Aren't we lucky to be out here!" she'd exclaim. "Just think, we could be home sitting in a chair, watching soap operas!" Spirit!

So there you have it. What's golf all about? It's about fortitude, grit, and courage. It's about willpower, resolve, and spirit, and dozens of other adjectives. Is it the game of golf that inspires you? Or is it the people who play golf that inspire you? Perhaps it can be a little bit of both. Either way, don't give up on this game. Not because of age, health, or even handicap. Get out there and feel the sun on your face and the breeze at your back. Find that lovely group of women friends who support you, inspire you, and make you want to laugh. It's worth it!

Joanie Gilmore

Going Bunkers

A bad attitude is worse than a bad swing.

Payne Stewart

Jamie Hullett may be small at first glance, but every-thing about her golf game is big. Five feet, two inches on her tiptoes, she struggles to get her weight up to ninety pounds. When she answers the phone in her high-pitched, tiny voice, people ask to speak to her parents. But this girl is from the big state of Texas. She has a big heart and big dreams. On top of that, when she swings, she uses every ounce of her being to smash the ball.

When we toured on the Pro Am for the Betty Puskar Futures Classic, she and I met up at the Pines Country Club in Morgantown, West Virginia. Each team of four amateurs, mostly males, was paired with one professional. I was playing in the group behind Jamie as they waited for the seventeenth tee.

A par three, the hole plays every bit of 200 yards and calls for a three or five wood. Sitting slightly above the green, the tee overlooks a steep valley with tall, old oak trees surrounding the hole. With soft sand bunkers on

every side, the green slopes from back to front. Because of
the severe slope and quickness of the green, making an
up-and-down from anywhere is difficult. By far, this is the
toughest hole on the course, and it often gets backed up.

"Hey, Jamie," I walked closer, "how's it going?"

"You wouldn't believe this guy I'm playing with," she
hissed under her breath. She inclined her head in his
direction. A brawny six feet, three inches, he completely
dwarfed my petite friend.

"Why?" I asked. "What's up?"

"You know, he's one of *those*."

I did know. We all knew. Every professional female
golfer has met him at some point in her career. Overly
confident, too proud, God's gift to the golfing world. The
type of male who automatically assumes himself better
than any woman on the course.

"You should hear this guy. 'I hit it farther than the pro. I
hit it farther than the pro,'" Jamie mimicked him in sing-
song. "He taunts me over each lousy, extra yard. It's so
juvenile."

"Bragging over a yard? At his size, he should be pounding it by you. What a jerk."

"It's a good thing we have only two more holes to play,"
she admitted. "I've just about had it with him."

We watched while all four amateurs in her group teed off.
None of them came close to hitting the green, including Mr.
Super Golfer. He dribbled it off the tee only sixty yards.

Although clearly embarrassed, he turned to Jamie and
sneered, "We wanted to give you the opportunity to hit a
good one, since we've been carrying you all day."

Jamie seethed in silence. Then, determined to meet his
challenge, she yanked a club from her bag and whispered
to me, "Guys like him should be nicer to someone who can
put a ball anywhere she wants. See that deep bunker on
the left? Just watch."

Jamie strolled to the tee, took dead aim, and belted her ball. It soared yards past his and landed exactly where she intended—buried as an unplayable lie, deep in the face of the sand bunker.

The others on her team groaned with disappointment and disgust. But, as she walked off the tee, Jamie dropped me a long, slow wink of sweet satisfaction. A perfectly executed sabotage. Sometimes, just to prove a point, you need one of *those*.

Kristen Samp and Jamie Hullett

Golf Lessons

If it doesn't matter if you win or lose, but how you play the game, why do they keep score?
    Charley Boswell, Professional Blind Golfer

How can one activity cause so many different emotions to spill out of a woman? How can love turn to hate in an instant, then back to love again? No, I am not speaking about romantic love! I am referring to the game of golf!

There is nothing like a beautiful golf course to make a woman feel at peace with herself and with God.

My favorite color, green, surrounded me many times as I stood looking out over the golf course preparing to perfect my swing—one more time! Oops! One more time, ONE MORE time, ONE MORE TIME!

"I HATE this game of golf!" I swore off golf more times than I would like to remember! But the next sunny day found me being pulled, by some force beyond my control, to the fairways and the greens of our local golf course.

Like some people having an illicit affair, I found pleasure in the very thing that was causing me pain! Yet, I kept going back for more.

I loved the warm feeling the sun provided as I walked the course. I loved the feeling of satisfaction I got from the persistence of perfecting my swing. I loved the solitude when I was alone, and the bonding found with Ladies' Day outings. I loved the power I found in the swing of my husband's arms when we golfed together and the camaraderie when we played with other couples. I loved seeing a beginning golfer and knowing I wasn't alone in my pursuit to improve.

But most of all I appreciated the perseverance I learned in going back each time to continue improving my game. For it is that same persistence that has afforded me the will to persevere in life after my golfing days ended due to multiple sclerosis, which I now live with.

There are many activities that teach us about life, but in golf the training we are taught far exceeds the lessons of any other game. With its ups and downs, its penalties and rewards, its beauty and roughs, golf instills in us many lessons we need in the game of life.

Now I spend my days on a three-wheel motorized scooter because I can no longer walk. The strength in my arms has greatly diminished, and the sun now saps every bit of my strength. But the beauty and persistence and other lessons I found on the golf course cannot be taken from me.

When I fall, when exhaustion overtakes me, and when I feel I can't go on, I persevere in spite of the penalties. Looking around I see there are others so much worse off than me. I do so appreciate golf lessons.

Betty King

"Seeing I had already hit you once,
was I correct in yelling EIGHT!?"

"Tee Time"

My mother loves tea. When I was growing up, one of her favorite escapes was a hot cup of tea and a good book; it was simple deliverance from the dramatic sibling squabbles and the rote chores of laundry, cooking, and cleaning. It was the perfect release after a long day, or whenever she needed to relax. As I got older we'd sip tea during our mother/daughter chats; she'd settle into the couch and wrap her hands around a mug, absorbing the warmth, as I absorbed her wisdom and advice.

Though I am now married, when my mom comes to visit, we still have our tea time. It is a family ritual of connection in which I am the beneficiary of sage bits of knowledge that help me navigate the roads of life. One of our midnight tea times a few years back was especially life-changing.

"I'm so tired, Mom," I told her. "I feel like all I do is change diapers and chase kids. Being a mom is so hard. I don't know how you did it."

"Well, it's tough," she agreed, "but it sounds like you need time for yourself. Do you have some time when you can get away and do something you enjoy?"

"Not really," I replied, with frustration welling up in my

voice. "Pete works late almost every day and plays golf on Saturdays, so I can't really do anything. But I don't want to deny him that time because he works hard and deserves a break, too."

"Why don't you go with him?" she asked.

"I dunno. I guess it never occurred to me. What would we do with the kids?"

"Find a sitter," she said, smiling and taking a sip of tea.

Her words gave me the permission I needed. Though it took some footwork and planning, I arranged for a caregiver for our daughters and got serious about my game.

Saturday golf now helps my marriage and gives me a much-needed break from the "mommy routine." I golf on a regular basis, creating opportunities to practice and play whenever I can. The velvety greens, the rolling hills, and fresh air offer me a true escape. When I'm concentrating on my game, I don't ponder my to-do list. After taking "me" time, I can better handle a bustling household of activity and toddler tantrums with a fresh perspective— just like my mom.

Looking back, my mother's teatime habit was simple self-nurturing. My "tee" times are too. I look forward to when my daughters and I have chats over a cup of tea or on the tee box. And I'll tell them how "teatime" with Grandma . . . became "tee time" for me.

Celeste T. Palermo

2

MORE THAN A GAME

Theme: Self-Revelation and Insight

There is not a single hole that can't be birdied if you just think. But there is not one that can't be double-bogeyed if you ever stop thinking.

Bobby Jones

Play It

Life is like a game of golf,
It starts with small beginnings,
And some folks play for fun and laughs
And some folks play for winnings.
But one thing's true of either goal,
The yardstick is the same:
In life—and golf—what matters most
Is how you play the game.

Joan Paquette

Follow Through

If I could wish for my life to be perfect, it would be tempting, but I would have to decline, for life would no longer teach me anything.

Allyson Jones

"I don't want to go! How stupid, pushing little white balls around with a stick? Whoever heard of playing eighteen holes as a final exam?" I fumed at my mom.

"Sallie, you have to go," she reminded me. "Your sister plays golf all the time and she'd love to take you out on the course."

"I think I'd rather flunk out right now than play that dumb game," I said as I stomped off to my room.

Mom was right. I did have to take the final. And my sister, Gloria, was a semipro golfer, so she'd probably want to get it over with quick and painlessly. Playing with me wasn't going to be a cakewalk for her. She might even let me take a couple of mulligans to end the game faster.

The Saturday of my final arrived and Gloria appeared at our door bright and early. How could she look so chipper and pulled together in her red, white, and blue ensemble at 5 A.M.? I trudged to the car like a woman condemned to death.

We pulled into Meadowlark Golf Course in her convertible and she unloaded her Calloways and put her golf shoes on. I admit she did look like a pro. I got my rental clubs and headed for the first tee.

"Whoa there, Sis," Gloria called out. "If you're taking your final, you're doing it in style. We're getting a cart and you're driving."

A cart and I'm driving. Now this is getting interesting, I thought. *Maybe I'll even get to yell, "Fore!"*

We hopped in the cart, bags of clubs in the back, and with a jerk took off for the first tee. I felt very grown-up; we were playing with the big boys now.

"Head down, hips first, knees bent, let your arms glide along after your shoulders. Always remember to follow through," Gloria coached me.

"I'm tryin', Sis, but this isn't as easy as it looks. The follow-through is hard."

"Took me awhile to get the hang of it, too," she said with a knowing smile.

Why did I feel as though we weren't talking golf anymore?

"I only took golf as a college elective because all the guys in the dance class were geeks," I confessed to my sister.

"I know, Mom told me," she replied. "I'm proud of you taking a Saturday off from your friends to finish your class. Do you know why I started playing this game?"

"No," I admitted. "I thought you loved golfing."

"Oh, I do now. But in the beginning this was the only place where I could go to be alone. Just me; no kids, no husband, no house, no phone. Out here I'm only responsible for me. I have a good time, then I go back home refreshed and ready to follow through, so to speak."

I thought about that for a moment and the different

reasons people golf. All of a sudden it didn't seem like such a stupid game after all.

Now, I won't lie and say I took up golf after that day, so many years ago. I still prefer to dance rather than play eighteen holes. My sister went on to win many golf tournaments before she lost her life to cancer. But I learned one thing that day—in golf, as in life, you always have to follow through.

Sallie A. Rodman

"What did we ever do before cell phones?"

The Nineteenth Hole

In golf, as in life, you get out of it what you put into it.

Sam Snead

My dad worked an average of fourteen hours per day, six to seven days a week, for over thirty-five years. Time for a hobby or leisure activity? Never! Who would have the time for such nonsense?

He immigrated to America from Greece at the very young age of fourteen years. His hard work and dedication resulted in the ownership of liquor and delicatessen stores in New Jersey. He was proud of his accomplishments and what he could provide for his family.

That is why what happened next was so out of character for him. I was the youngest child, the only daughter, and the first in the family to complete college. Dad was very proud when he attended my graduation in 1961.

Prior to commencement activities, Dad approached me and asked quietly, "Are you really graduating?"

"Yes, of course, why are you asking, Dad?"

He looked so serious, I became frightened. Maybe he or

Mom was sick, or something had happened to my brother. . . . "Dad, what is wrong, what is going on?"

Dad smiled and started to laugh. "Well, if you are graduating, my job is over. I have educated my children and provided for all of you. I am going to sell the store and retire."

"Great, but what will you do? I only know you behind the counter of a store, slicing meats and cheese, cooking in the kitchen, and serving customers. I can't imagine you doing anything else," I said.

He stared straight ahead and stated with authority, "I am going to play golf!"

"Golf? You are going to play golf? You have never played golf. I never heard you mention golf. Have you ever taken a lesson? Have you ever been on a golf course? Do you have golf clubs?" The questions came tumbling out of my mouth with no opportunity for him to respond. I was shocked but also relieved. No one was sick. There was no immediate or looming crisis. Just golf, Dad was going to play golf!

And so began Dad's love affair with the game of golf. He taught my brother and me the game and instilled his enthusiasm in us. Dad would look at us and say, "If you live your life as you play the game of golf, you will be fine."

He repeated often, "Stay focused and hit straight down the fairway. When you get to the green, concentrate, don't get distracted, and know where you want to put the ball. Do this and you will reach your goals. However, always remember to take time to enjoy the nineteenth hole."

Dad wanted us to have goals and to stay focused on them to realize success. He also wanted us to enjoy ourselves, take time to have fun with friends and family, and keep our priorities in order. He encouraged me not to hide behind my womanhood but to realize I could be whatever I wanted to be—including a solid woman golfer!

He always took time to smell the roses and enjoy everything that comprised his "nineteenth hole." Dad retired at the age of fifty-six and played nine to eighteen holes of golf every day until his death at the age of eighty-six. What a great role model!

Dad, I am still playing golf and think of you whenever I tee off. I know you are playing right along with me. I have, and will continue to strive to always have, the time for the important things in life. Thank you, Dad, for teaching me the importance of the "nineteenth hole."

Helen Xenakis

My Dream Job

For as far back as I can remember, Saturdays were reserved for my dad. He and his buddies played the same tee time, at the same public golf course, virtually every week for my entire childhood. I was also there every Saturday, heading to the course just to spend time with him. When I got older, I started playing pretty well. The head pro kept an eye on me as I chipped, putted, and practiced during Dad's five-hour rounds. My favorite part was when he made the turn and stopped by to hand me my favorite bean burrito for lunch. The two-minute conversation we would have about my morning practice carried me through the next two and a half hours. I loved every minute of it. While my friends spent their weekends at the mall and the beach, I gladly spent my free time honing my skills and hoping to be invited to play the last three holes as a fivesome. With the course we played being nearly forty minutes from home, we always spent the car ride talking, laughing, crying, encouraging, scheming, and dreaming.

My summers gradually became more involved. My dad often played hookie from work to watch me play the last few holes in my near-daily tournaments. Those summer nights were filled with sweet memories for me. We watched so many sunsets reflecting the colors of the rainbow on glistening dewdrops as they settled on the many blades of grass. I can still remember the smell of the freshly cut turf and the feel of moisture seeping into our socks as we made footprints in the just-watered fairways. During my high school years, I learned algebra from my dad as we worked out my scoring average and my greens hit in regulation.

The time finally came to leave home for school. I chose my dad's alma mater, Arizona State University. We no longer had our Saturdays together, but my folks visited often enough, and my dad and I talked almost every Saturday afternoon.

When I was in college I struggled to make the traveling team. Although I was good enough to be a member of a national championship team, I was disappointed that my hard work wasn't paying off. I couldn't help but feel like I was letting my dad down. It became apparent that if I couldn't beat my own teammates, I would never play on the Ladies Professional Golf Association (LPGA) tour.

So, instead, I worked in just about every aspect of the golf profession. I worked at many golf courses. I learned to teach people to play the game. I coached at the high school, Division III, and even Division I collegiate levels. My résumé includes several Coach of the Year awards and countless other accomplishments. Still, I never felt I lived up to "our" dreams for me. I knew deep down he wanted me to be an LPGA Tour player, and I simply was never good enough.

Now my dad has passed away and I have children of my own. Although they are young, we go to our backyard now and then and put a plastic golf ball down and hand my son a silly little blue plastic "wood." I cheer and shout when he makes contact, then I run after the ball and encourage him to keep trying again and again. One day, for no particular reason, I finally understood what "job" my dad really wanted for me. It wasn't the LPGA and it wasn't stardom. I was sitting there in the baking sun that afternoon doing the perfect "job." I was being my son's mom, and golf was the perfect tool to do it. I was spending time with him, talking, laughing, crying, encouraging, scheming, and dreaming. I was truly living the legacy Dad had given me. All his teachings and all his wisdom came through my cheers and pats on the shoulder and hugs. My sons are lucky to have had a grandfather like him. His legacy lives through me. I hope my sons figure out in their lives, long before I figured out, that playing golf with me will be the legacy I will leave them. No expectations, no wishes for stardom . . . just a Saturday afternoon, hanging out with Mom.

Tana Figueras Thomas

Be-Attitude

Don't compromise yourself. You are all you've got.

Janis Joplin

For as long as I can remember, I treasured my time spent alone on the driving range, just me and endless golf balls to launch. And the feel of hitting that one perfect shot out of a hundred hooked me. As early as third grade, I'd written an essay called, "What I Want to Be When I Grow Up." And what I dreamed of being, even then, was a member of the Ladies Professional Golf Association (LPGA).

Merely a year after graduating from college, I competed on the Asian and Futures Tours. I earned my nonexempt status at the LPGA Final Qualifying Tournament the same year. I was living my dream. But by then, I'd already been diagnosed with a debilitating disease called interstitial cystitis (IC).

As a naive young woman, I accepted the doctor's flat announcement: "There's no cure. You'll just have to learn to live with it." So I tried to. For years. But the effort consumed me.

A chronic, inflammatory bladder condition, IC's symptoms are severe and unrelenting. It felt like paper cuts lined my bladder wall. Tenderness and pressure in the pelvic area meant that every step I took was painful and, for a golfer, pure torture. At times, I couldn't even bend down to line up a putt. And the frequent urgency to urinate—as often as fifty times a day—interfered with my game. The agony of a full bladder made me desperate. Instead of focusing on a shot, I fretted about making it to the next Porta John.

Playing golf on the LPGA Tour requires travel, up to thirty or thirty-five weeks per year. And travel involved both dread and deceit. I demanded an aisle seat on the plane—and would spend an entire flight devising excuses for visiting the restroom. Too much coffee. Cleaning my contact lenses. Brushing my teeth. I covered my tracks as thoroughly as a drug addict.

I suffered socially, never telling even my closest friends about IC. Sharing a room with any of the ladies on tour was impossible. The need to urinate forced me into an exhaustive twenty-minute sleep cycle and, eventually, eleven years of sleep deprivation. I cut off friendships; I kept people from getting too close.

The disease hindered my golf game, too, wreaking havoc with my performance. Several times I had to withdraw from tournaments in the middle of a round because I needed to leave the course for a toilet.

Saddest of all, IC affected my personal life. It controlled my days and consumed my thoughts. It took its toll on my marriage. It numbed me to the joys of parenting my daughter. It stole my happiness and my personality.

And yet, through it all, I continued to play golf.

In some respects, the LPGA was my lifeline, a substitute reality. Each time I stood at the tee, I was a kid again—absorbed in the pure ecstasy of hitting balls, my worst problem the possibility of an afternoon thunderstorm.

For nearly twelve years, captive to the condition, I pretended to be whole and healthy. The perfect athlete striving to hit the perfect ball to win the perfect game.

And then the thunderstorm rolled in.

Anger at the disease. Exhaustion from coping. Despair at going on. I hit rock bottom and came face-to-face with failure. I searched for a way out. Out of pain, out of suffering, out of life.

Fortunately for me, I looked up. And help arrived: a wonderful doctor and a miracle drug.

After nearly twelve years in a downward spiral, I began to surface. Over a period of months, the drug kicked in and the IC symptoms abated. I gained a new interest in life and a new enthusiasm for golf. I was finally performing symptom-free.

But the wins and tour titles that followed paled next to the victory of reclaiming my role as wife and mother. I'd found myself again and reveled in the discovery. I realized I didn't need to be best, to be perfect. It was enough to simply be.

I became the primary spokesperson for interstitial cystitis.

I became a visible champion for its cause.

I became passionate about reaching out to other women and offering them hope.

Retired now from the LPGA, I've been propelled to a new place, a new plan, a new purpose. At last, I've found perfection . . . in just being.

Terry-Jo Myers

Tunnel Vision

It's not enough just to swing at the ball. You've got to loosen your girdle and let 'er fly.

Babe Zaharias

I loved everything about that day.

The summer sky. The spectacular course. The eager crowd.

It was the Fourth of July and I was in Portland, Oregon, competing in the U.S. Women's Open, the biggest event on the tour. As a nineteen-year-old rookie, I adored playing to the huge galleries—of at least one hundred thousand people—and I fed on their energy and enthusiasm. The sparkly, patriotic "USA" tattoo on my left arm winked in the sunlight. Everyone's excitement was contagious and my smile constant.

I did, after all, have a lot to smile about.

For three days, I'd played great and positioned myself to win. I'd been hitting well and was in a good spot mentally. I had a lot riding on this opportunity. In fourth place going into the final round, I felt focused when I stepped up to the eighteenth tee with the same confidence as I'd approached the last seventy-one holes. I was cruising.

I sighted down the tee box, the narrow fairway, the green. It was a comfortable par five.

I visualized my drive, took my famous quirky backswing, and carried through for the same quality result I'd come to expect.

Whack.

But this time it didn't land where I planned. It drifted off course—and straight into a hazard. My second shot? Back into the hazard.

It played out like a *Tin Cup* scenario. I finally putted in for a nine.

A nine.

I'd rarely had a seven, never even an eight. And now I ended the Open on a nine. The worst hole I ever played as a professional golfer.

I was dazed. Devastated. Discouraged. I wanted to make myself as small as the ball and crawl right into the cup with it.

All the workouts, all the practicing, all the dedication I'd put toward this tournament . . . my vision of winning . . . gone. Stunned, I turned away from the hole.

My dad waited for me to come off the green. He came inside the ropes and pulled me close for a bear hug. "It's okay, Natalie," he consoled, "you gave it everything you had." He tugged on my long, blond braid. "There'll be other days and other events, you know."

Other events? Like this one? My chin sank onto my chest.

"The sun will come up tomorrow," he insisted. "You'll see."

I shrugged. I just wanted to get away, to be alone, to work through the numbness. To plant one foot ahead of the other along the hollow tunnel of defeat and get to the locker room as quickly as possible so I could sulk in private. But when I raised my head, I noticed all the fans lining both sides of the cordoned path, waving and calling out to me.

It was a cheering crowd that wanted an autograph.

My autograph.

"Natalie, we love you!" someone shouted.

"Would you take a picture with me?" a teenager begged.

"You're our favorite!" another cheered.

They all wanted a piece of me. They wanted a moment of my time, a slice of my attention. Suddenly, I realized I had a choice to make, and, after a short pause of deliberation, I chose to face my fans. Up to this time, I'd prided myself in staying connected to my gallery and making it a practice after each event to be present until the last slip of paper was signed, every person greeted, and all the pictures snapped. Stiffening my shoulders, I decided this day would be no different.

Taking a deep breath, I smoothed my black Adidas dress, pasted a big smile on my lips, and reached for the pen a woman passed to me. *"Natalie Gulbis,"* I scratched stiffly and tried to focus on the next beckoning, outstretched hand. And the next. And the next.

Then it hit me as powerfully as a long drive. *No one cared that I hadn't won.*

How I did—or didn't do—on the last hole made no difference to them. These people were here for the love of the game, the enjoyment of the sport, and the thrill of the event. And, most importantly, they were there to support me.

"You are such an inspiration to my daughter," a woman praised.

"We love you!" someone hollered.

"We'll be following you," another declared.

My hand paused in midair. The roar around me stilled. And in that split second, I recognized that we shared the same passion, these wonderful people and I: the love of the game, the joy of golf. I realized how fortunate I was to reach this pinnacle of success, to play professionally, and to follow my dream. Eagerly, now, I wove my way, from side to side, along the gallery of fans. *"Natalie Gulbis,"* I scribbled with a flourish.

As a peaceful satisfaction swept over me, I smiled inwardly. More than ever before, I felt grateful and privileged to be present until each paper was autographed, every hand shaken, and the last photograph taken.

Natalie Gulbis

In the Zone

Yes, golf has been my savior, there is no doubt about it.

Annika Sörenstam

"The scores were astronomical but . . ."

That was the lead for an article in our local paper, the *Staten Island Advance*, covering a golf tournament I had played in during my high school years. One of our gym teachers was an avid golfer, and she started a golf club, which I joined with my best friend. We may not have turned into prize-winning players, but we certainly enjoyed the experience, because we went to great lengths to get on the links on our own.

We didn't have clubs, and we didn't have much money, and we didn't live close to the golf course, but we did have plenty of time and enthusiasm. We'd borrow an old set of clubs from my friend's boyfriend (and I mean old—if we slid the clubs too hardily into the bag, they would fall out the holes in the canvas), walk a couple of miles to Silver Lake Golf Course, go to the pro shop, and rent a bag and a putter. Then we would split the clubs and head off to play eighteen holes. Perhaps we offered amusement to the spectators on the club veranda overlooking the first hole, but we braved the scrutiny, drove our balls, and headed off for the other, less observed seventeen holes.

It was great fun and I liked golf, but I didn't "get it." By that I mean that beyond being with friends, being out in pleasant weather, and engaging in a sport, I didn't understand the heart of the game, that which makes it so compelling.

Some time later, after not playing golf for years because I had babies to care for and little time, I was able to return to the links. My husband was a civilian employee of the Department of the Army and we were stationed in Germany for four years. While out of the United States, we lived on an army base and participated in army life. We were fortunate to be able to go to Golf Week in Berchtesgaden, a beautiful area in the Bavarian Alps.

At that time of my life, I had responsibilities, worries, anxiety. We had a big family, and those kids were, of course, always on my mind. Then we played golf.

Child care was provided. The younger children went to the on-site child care center, while the older kids had many activities to keep them busy and amused.

We played golf in an area where, by just turning our heads to the right, we saw the scenic Alpine setting where *The Sound of Music* had been filmed. We played golf on an uncrowded course where the satisfying "thwack" of a ball being hit by a driver could be heard loud and clear.

One day it started to pour, so my husband and I rushed to the pro shop, bought Windbreakers, and finished playing the entire course.

We had a week of golf lessons in Berchtesgaden, culminating in another tournament. This time the scores did not soar to the heavens, and this time I actually won a trophy!

And, when I played, I forgot I had a bunch of kids, tons of responsibilities, and financial worries. I thought about that little white ball and how to approach it, and my mind was focused. Of course, if the kids had needed me or there was any problem, I would have put down the club and hastened to them, but the point is they didn't need me every minute. They were having fun, and for a short period of time, I could just relax and have fun myself. Maybe it was like a form of meditation because of the absolute focus.

So while I enjoyed the scenery, being outdoors, being with friends, and engaging in a game, I realized golf allows the player to zone out on everyday concerns and zone in on an engrossing pastime. That was when I knew what golf was really all about. That was when I "got it."

Carolyn Ford

Hot Shot

If you obey all the rules, you miss all the fun.

Katharine Hepburn

When I was five, I loved the sound of metal spikes click-ing against the cement cart paths at the club where my dad played golf. Once, I stepped on an empty coke can and it stuck to the bottom of my shoe. I thought it sounded like I had on spikes, so I clomped around in it for hours. Now, I could be a golfer just like my dad. The only thing missing, I decided, was my own set of clubs.

That Christmas, wrapping paper littered the floor. All the gifts had been opened and I eyed my eight-year-old brother with envy. There Swen stood, swinging the cut-down clubs he'd gotten for Christmas. Then, one at a time, he put them in his new golf bag.

"Say, Perry," my dad's voice held a promise, "you have one more present."

I turned a doubtful gaze at the bare space under the tree.

"Really," he insisted, "but it takes a scavenger hunt to find it." He grabbed my hand. "Let's go look."

The entire family followed as Dad led us through the house giving hints.

We found it hiding beneath my bed—black and fluorescent yellow, "Daisy" was spelled down the side in bold letters. Inside the miniature bag was an old Ping Answer putter along with a wedge, seven iron, and driver—all cut down to perfectly fit a five-year-old. Elated, I lugged the bag everywhere, convinced it made me look professional.

After school each day, the two of us would go to the driving range. I stood behind him and mimicked every move he made in his admirable, fluid swing. By the next year, Dad and I were playing in the club parent/child championships. He played from the blue tees; I teed off from the 150-yard markers.

"Awesome shot, Perry," he would congratulate me. Or, "Wow! You put some muscle into that drive."

A scratch amateur player who competed in national events, he carried our team for many years. Yet he always made me believe that the shot I hit was the difference-maker in every tournament we played.

Thanks to him, my competitive love for the game grew. The two of us pooled our talents to enter national father/daughter events. We took three titles before I turned professional.

At one tournament, we were coming down the stretch—three under par—playing in pure, alternate-shot format. Dad lagged a putt on the seventeenth hole within six inches of the hole.

"Your turn, Perry," he said.

It was a simple tap-in. A piece of cake. A shot anybody could make.

I grabbed my club with my left hand and sauntered across the green. Leaning out over one foot, I casually flicked it in with the wrong side of the putter. And the world went into slow motion.

The ball hit the edge of the cup. It began a painfully . . . precarious . . . spin. Around the entire circumference of the lip.

My breath caught. My heart stopped. My eyes bulged.

Until, finally, the ball rattled into the hole.

I gave a huge sigh of relief and turned away.

Dad's look was stern. "You can backhand as many putts as you want," he hissed, "but never, *never* when you play with *me.*"

We won the tournament. By a single stroke.

Since then, I've never backhanded a putt into any hole, even it if was hanging on the edge. I've learned the importance of one shot.

Perry Swenson

Making the Move

*If you prepare for months and months and set
high goals, the last thing to do is be in my own
way. There's two people in me; one calm and
one totally excited. The calm one won today.*

Annika Sörenstam

Candlestick Park was packed. Nearly all of San Francisco
was there to watch the 1989 World Series match between
the Giants and the Oakland A's. Friends and I were sharing
box seats when we felt the whole stadium sway.

Sliding open the window, I leaned out and cheered, "We
can make the earth move!" Little did I know.

The Loma Prieta earthquake—registering 7.1 on the
Richter scale—had just rocked the Santa Cruz Mountains
and devastated the Bay area.

As team players rounded up family members and sup-
porters ran onto the field, a security guard escorted us
through the stands, onto the field, and out through the
locker rooms. The parking lot was a madhouse. It took
frantic hours to get out.

Meanwhile, the Bay Bridge collapsed, the Cypress freeway pancaked onto its lower deck, and buildings shattered. Gas lines and water pipes broke. The quake knocked out all power. San Francisco was dark; the streets eerie and empty.

It took nearly five hours to navigate a two-mile trip. Because the freeway south was closed, we made an early exit and spent the night with Julie Inkster. Her house sustained considerable damage . . . which made me fearful of what I would find at my own.

After a restless night, we got an early start. Landslides, fissures, fires . . . like golf course hazards one after another. The forty-five-minute drive took us *nine hours.*

Heart racing at the sight of my ravaged neighborhood, I pulled into the driveway and marveled at the appearance of my own home. "We dodged the bullet!" I exclaimed in awe.

But the inside told a different story.

Shards of glass.

Toppled shelves.

Shattered furniture.

The entire house had moved six inches off its front foundation. Bedroom doors were skewed and jammed. Appliances, artwork, glassware . . . all destroyed. Shattered golf trophies—so important to me just hours ago . . . a lifetime ago . . . littered the floors.

Numbed by devastation, I gawked at the rubble. *What if?* I wondered, knowing I might not have survived had I been home when the earthquake struck.

Knowing the house was unsafe, I slept that night on the lawn. With my ear to the ground, I heard aftershocks roll in like the waves in Monterey Bay. They just . . . kept . . . coming.

After five nights of "camping out," reality smacked me in the face . . . along with persistent rain that now pelted from the sky. First things first.

A place to stay. Thank goodness for friends. And friends of friends.

Storage. For the things I might salvage. Not so easy . . . the entire city seemed to need it, too. My eager-to-help brother sent a van to take my stuff to Reno.

Sorting. Picking through possessions. Making decisions on what was salvageable and what I needed to haul to the dump. Truckloads went to the dump.

The work was as emotional as it was physical. For days, I mourned while I culled and cleaned with the same intensity as I had once chipped on the practice greens.

But I was in for aftershocks of an even more personal nature.

While arranging my move to Reno, stunning financial woes came to light when I closed checking accounts. Those I relied on to manage my money affairs had failed me. Once again, my world swayed: me, a professional golfer, and I found myself financially strapped. With no emotional stamina to investigate or hire an auditor, I felt as depleted as my bankbook.

Wearily, I returned for a final walk-through of my house and a last good-bye.

I sank onto the thick carpet. My fingers plucked at the nubby berber as I turned my eyes to the oversized windows and the gorgeous view they framed: the Santa Cruz Mountains sparkling in the same sunlight that warmed the greens at my favorite course.

I sobbed out loud.

My whole body vibrated with the intensity of my grief. Hugging knees to my chest, I mourned the loss of my home. I cried over my possessions. I despaired at my finances. Yet even as I wept, my tears streamed in sudden gratitude—for friends, family, and my personal safety.

All of this, my eyes swept the room where dozens of prized golf trophies once stood sentinel, *this is not important.*

Like a save shot, I felt a shift in my perspective and knew I must salvage myself from the rubble. I resolved to de-emphasize the trivial, appreciate others, laugh long, and live hearty. To survive. To achieve. To make the earth move.

Turning to golf—my only constant—I applied this new perspective to my career.

I practiced every day that winter. Thumbing my nose at the fickle Nevada weather, I forced myself out of bed and onto the greens—determined to combat the ever-threatening depression, focusing on specific goals. With a club in my grip, I began to repair and reclaim myself just as surely as the freeway work going on in the Bay area. And it paid off.

In January 1990, I won the first Ladies Professional Golf Association (LPGA) event of the new year, the Jamaica Classic. With money in my pocket, I was feeling more confident. I went on to play twenty-four tournaments and made the cut as many times, qualifying each week I played.

That year I scored my lowest average ever; I watched it go down a half-stroke every single round. I took sixteen top-ten places. And my purse fattened accordingly.

Thanks to kind friends and their friends, I received sound financial advice. I paid off loans for the earthquake reconstruction, sold the Santa Cruz house, and purchased another home in Reno. I gained a new sense of self-sufficiency and learned to manage my banking, books, and bills. While San Francisco rebuilt itself, I put my personal life in order.

Most importantly, I discovered that when the earth shifts beneath us, we must salvage the best in ourselves . . . and move on.

Patty Sheehan

Charting a New Course

The future belongs to those who believe in the beauty of their dreams.

Eleanor Roosevelt

When I was fifteen years old, I competed in a club championship—with my secondhand irons. At five holes down, I was being beaten . . . and beaten badly. But I shoved back thoughts of discouragement and refused to give up. My brow furrowed in concentration. Then, with six holes to play, my game started to pick up.

After winning four in a row, I approached the last hole with a degree of confidence. But it wasn't to be. An ancient, forty-year-old woman took the game.

Gulping down my disappointment while managing to muster a smile, I congratulated her and walked away.

My mother threw an arm around my shoulders. "I'm so proud of you." She squeezed me tight.

"But I lost."

"Ah, but I'm proud of the *way* you lost," she nodded. "No show of temper or disgust. You accepted your defeat with class. And I couldn't be prouder."

As a reward for my attitude, my parents bought me the new golf bag I'd been eyeing and lusting after—the golf bag of my dreams. The green and beige plaid one. The one with the light leather trim.

But the greater reward was the lesson I learned that day: Attitude is everything.

Attitude affects how we approach the game. It directly affects how we play. It proves our mettle when we're under pressure. In the larger picture, it affects our outlook on life in general.

My own attitude has stood me in good stead: I'm a trail-blazer. As a young girl, I was the lone female on our boys' baseball team. And I didn't grow up in the ranks. I was not on anyone's radar. In fact, I first played golf at four-hole weekend clinics—encouraged by those same boys I played ball with. By age thirteen, I embraced the game that would set the tone for the rest of my life.

In 1969, I was the Ladies Professional Golf Association (LPGA) Tour's Rookie of the Year, and—during my fifteen-year professional career—I went on to win twenty-seven events on the tour. I won the first Colgate Dinah Shore in 1972 and made 299 cuts in a row. I was definitely a competitor first and a golfer second! But I thrived during those golden years on the LPGA—traveling to foreign countries, playing with dignitaries, forging lifelong friendships. I felt fortunate to do what I loved to do most, golf.

But I wanted to go out while I was still on top, with no regrets, and my self-esteem still intact. I wanted to leave on my terms, and I wanted it to be my choice. When I made that momentous decision to retire, I took with me more than my titles and trophies: I took the life lessons the sport had taught me, determined to find a way to utilize them.

With that attitude, I approached a new game—finance. Upon entering the corporate world as a broker for Merrill-

Lynch, I recognized the sensibility of transferring my golf skills to business. I even thought them through and listed them:

Preparation. Chart the course and incorporate the aspects of practice.

Concentration. Focus on the tasks at hand.

Perseverance. Set unwavering goals and see them to the end.

Journey. Look at the totality, the whole, rather than short-term fixes.

Integrity. Base decisions on the common good, without compromise.

Patience. Stay calm in the face of adversity; learn from and don't repeat mistakes.

As I put these disciplines into practice, I recognized how their validity and value might impact others. Because golf had opened so many doors for me, I knew it could do the same for all women. With determination, I set out to blaze yet another trail.

I saw firsthand that golf courses are a prime setting for business deals, yet few women took advantage of the links to boost their careers. I wanted to offer Fortune 500 clients the opportunity for their female executives to use the game as an effective tool. To fulfill this need, I founded a golf event marketing and management company in 1989. The Jane Blalock Company (JBC) manages the Women's Legends Tour, LPGA Golf Clinics for Women, and the Jane Blalock Golf Academy.

Targeted at professional women, our programs enhance skills on and off the golf course. They help women become more at ease with golf as both a sport and a business tool. They explain the vocabulary, offer practical tips, and define the rules.

Understanding that golf gives women more confidence

in the marketplace and cements their footing in business relationships, we emphasize the networking and communications opportunities the game of golf provides. Our on-the-links programs teach etiquette, swing mechanics, course management, and—what else—positive mental attitude.

Golf, I've come to realize, is much more than a sport or a game. It is an Experience—with a capital E. It embodies all of our parts. It evokes all of our emotions. And it creates a full harmony of body, mind, and soul.

Golf taught me that no obstacle is bigger than my own determination. It taught me that the challenge—the quest—can overshadow pain, doubt, and fear. It taught me that where there is desire and will, anything can be overcome. Above all, golf showed me that I can be the master of my own fate.

And it is that can-be, can-do, can-reach attitude that I attempt to teach and share with other women. It's my trailblazing legacy. Then, someday, maybe they too will be rewarded with the golf bag of their dreams.

Perhaps green and beige plaid? With light leather trim?

Jane Blalock

On the Money

Though your beginning was insignificant, yet your end will increase greatly.

Job 8:7

Passion. Priority. Perseverance. Those are three important traits golf has taught me.

I started learning them by shagging balls for my dad at age five. Then I learned to play and took to the game. When I competed in my first junior golf tournament at age twelve, I knew I wanted to become a member of the Ladies Professional Golf Association (LPGA) one day. Passion.

After I turned pro right out of the University of California, Los Angeles (UCLA), I competed on the Futures Tour and went to Q-School . . . year after year after year. But it seemed I always missed the mark by one shot. On the advice of my coach, David Leadbetter, I headed to Europe, Japan, Australia, and Asia and improved my game. Priority.

Still, I'd set my sights on the LPGA, and, after nearly eighteen years, I reached my goal: I finally earned my conditional status. Perseverance.

But I remember one time, in particular, when all three characteristics came together for me.

After playing for three years on the LPGA Tour, I relocated to Scottsdale, Arizona. Although it was the perfect home base, I felt something was missing: a church home I could call my own. My search for a congregation came to a satisfying end when a flier appeared on my door one October day. It was an invitation to Desert Vista, a start-up church hosted, temporarily, at a local school.

As I attended and grew to love the people, especially the minister and his wife and family, I wanted to help the church grow. Over the next several years, determined to purchase property to build our own structure, we started a money-raising campaign called "Possess the Land." And to help achieve our goal, in 2002 I made a personal commitment of an additional $10,000 above my usual 10 percent tithe of my income.

Now, I was never a million-dollar tour winner, so pledging that much money was as much a challenge for me as Q-School had been only a few years prior! Even so, I felt an inner peace when I wrote a check for the first $1,000 installment at the beginning of the year. Fortunately, my new husband, Ken, supported my determination to reach the full amount.

Unfortunately, I wasn't playing well at the time. Still, as the 2002 season unfolded, I never doubted that God would fulfill my heart's desire.

I arrived in New York to play in the Wegman's Rochester International LPGA event, one of my favorite tour stops. Staying with my local housing family and dear friends, the DePetris, boosted my spirits. Another highlight of the week was the annual bowling tournament for players, caddies, and family members. Amid lots of laughing and good-natured teasing, my team—which included my mother— won Tuesday night. And my share of the pot was $200.

Well, it's a start, I shook my head. Huh. A drop in the bucket. I knew I was a long way from my financial goal.

On Thursday morning, I teed it up in the Wegman's tournament. Finally, I was playing well—shooting 68, 75, and 72—taking me into Sunday's round in the top ten. The week was looking up.

That Sunday morning I stood on the first tee, uttering my personal Jabez prayer, as I do before every round. I thanked God for the talent he blessed me with and the opportunity I had to be there, playing professionally . . . and playing well.

I asked God to let me feel pure, eternal peace throughout the game so I would truly enjoy the moment and be aware of the beauty of my surroundings.

I prayed to stay focused, in the present, one shot at a time.

And then I added a little extra to my customary prayer. I got specific.

"Please, God," I prayed, "help me remain obedient to my pledge. Reward me with a top-five finish so that I can send the remaining money to Desert Vista Church and glorify you. Amen."

Focused and present, I went on to play a fairly solid round. I had a great up-and-down on number eighteen, pitching a small wedge from about thirty yards to within four feet of the hole. I made the putt and shot a sixty-nine.

Not bad, I nodded in satisfaction. But was it good enough?

As I waited for the final few groups to finish, I watched both Juli Inkster and Beth Daniel surprisingly bogey number eighteen—putting them one shot behind me. My heart rate accelerated. When I saw the final results, goosebumps danced down my arms. But a sacred warmth flooded my heart.

My prayer had been heard. I finished in the top five.

In fact, I finished in fourth place solo, while four others—Rosales, Alfredson, Daniel, and Inkster—tied for fifth. I felt a sense of accomplishment that I knew was achieved solely and completely through the grace of God.

But it wasn't until I tallied my earnings that I understood the full scope of my blessings.

When I added my LPGA paycheck for fourth place to my DSW and Titleist sponsor bonuses and—yes—the piddling $200 I'd won bowling, my earnings totaled exactly $90,000.

Bingo!

My prayer had been answered. God rewarded me tenfold for my commitment to him. So awed and humbled was I by this realization of his providence that I mailed my tithe plus a $9,000 check for the remainder of my *entire* pledge amount to the church the very next day.

Once again, I was grateful for the life lessons learned through golf. I had set the church as my *priority*, I played the game with *passion*, and I *persevered* in the face of looming odds.

But God wasn't done with me.

It wasn't long before Ken and I discovered we'd conceived our daughter that wonderful week. Another answer to my prayers!

Kristal Parker-Manzo

FORE!warned Is Forearmed

If you really want to know what kind of man you're dating, get him out on the golf course.

On the golf course, personalities switch gears faster than Mario Andretti. A man who is sweet and patient when assembling an Ikea bookshelf can turn into Attila the Hun when armed with a metal stick and told to hit a little ball with it.

Take Paul. Paul had treated me to several nice dinners, and I was starting to think he was "the one." That is, until he hit his drive into the grass on the side of the fairway. Without switching clubs he strode purposely into the foot-tall wavy grass. He took a vicious swipe. The ball dribbled forward a foot or two. Another stride, another swipe. Dribble. Stride, Swipe, Dribble. He looked like a mad pineapple harvester brandishing his machete. The harder he swiped, the softer it dribbled.

When the ball came out of the grass, six strokes later, Paul fumed back to the cart. He held his driver aloft and smashed it down on a rock. Smash! Smash! Sm . . . whoops. The head of his new driver snapped off. Without missing a beat, he got in the cart. I picked up the driver head and scurried after him. I proffered it to him as we drove—these things can be reshafted. He chucked it into the water hazard.

I flashed on our future, picturing what would happen to me if Paul caught me using his razor to shave my legs. I avoided his calls until the phone stopped ringing.

And then there was Dan. Dan was great fun on our first dates—hiking along the coast and tailgating at baseball games. I could see myself with Dan. But then we went golfing.

I hit my drive, and it was uninspired. Dan drove the cart to my ball, but before I could get out, he scooped up my ball and threw it down the fairway toward the hole.

"What was that?!" I cried.

He shrugged, "You didn't seem happy with your shot, so I was just helping you."

"Please don't do that—I won't improve if I don't play fair," I explained. I plunked down a ball where mine had been and hit my second shot. Dan didn't utter another word to me—not one—for the remaining sixteen holes.

I returned the favor by not returning his calls—not one.

Now, Jim was a man's man, so we almost always golfed with his two best buddies. We had our routine down pat. We'd drive to the men's tee, get out of our carts, stand in silence like soldiers at attention while each of the men adjusted his stance, took ten or twelve practice shots, and then launched his drive. We only broke the silence to pay our compliments. When they were done, we'd get back in our two carts.

And we'd drive—zip, zip—right past the ladies' tee. I'd politely clear my throat and Jim would say, "What? Oh, yeah. Hey, guys! GUYS!" They'd look back in irritation from halfway down the fairway. Oh, yeah, the chick's gotta hit. They'd turn the carts back reluctantly.

As I got out of the cart Jim would say, "We're running a

little behind, so you better hurry." I'd hustle to the tee box. With the three formerly silent soldiers roughhousing loudly behind me, I'd hit my shot. Despite the din and the rush, it would be a decent shot, and I'd turn to Jim to collect my accolades. He'd be looking the other way. "Did you hit?" he'd ask.

When I finally gave up on Jim, I like to think he was pained when I forwarded his calls straight to voicemail, but I doubt he could hear that from the Hooters pay phone.

Then came the drinkers and the gamblers—men who not only wagered on the outcome of every shot, hole, and game, but who had side bets on whether the hawk wheeling overhead was stalking a gopher or a snake.

The drinkers spent even more money than the gamblers, stocking three beers at a time from the bar cart. Great fun, every one of them, but I wasn't keen on a future of serving burgers in a fast-food joint in my seventies because my husband had gambled and drunk our savings away.

Bob told me he hated world travel—a passion of mine—because "every city has the same thing" (streets and buildings)—but he never missed the opportunity to visit a new golf course because they were each so different.

Todd told me on Monday that he couldn't afford the $250 flight to Phoenix to visit his father who'd just been diagnosed with cancer, but called me excitedly on Tuesday to say he'd gotten a tee time at Pebble Beach, where the green fees are $400.

It wasn't hard to imagine a life with any of these guys. Paul would explode the first time I shrank one of his shirts. Dan would pout and give me the silent treatment if I didn't like his DVD choice. Jim might get carried away with his buddies at a party and forget to drive me home. With Bob I would never travel east of the Mississippi—or west, for that matter. Todd would pack me off to an assisted-care facility—make that a state-run assisted-care facility—the minute I got a hangnail.

I started to question my brilliant man-weeding scheme. Perhaps the hurdle was too high. I was running out of single men.

And then I golfed with David. David received and dealt compliments with equal grace. He was chatty between holes and quiet when he needed to be. He paid attention during my shots and protected me from the occasional errant shots from other fairways. He bought my lunch and at the end of the game, over beers on the club deck, we toasted a perfect day.

Today is another perfect day, and I should be out on the golf course—but I don't want to be too far from the phone when David calls.

Diana Fairbanks DeMeo

"Golf is deceptively simple and endlessly complicated . . . like dating."

3

A GAME FOR ALL GENERATIONS

Theme: Friends and Family

I started golf at eight. Dad had an auto body repair shop. He and Mom sacrificed all the time. Every extra cent was used to get me into amateur tournaments. They gave up things to make sure I had clothes that looked nice. They would go without, so I could have three new balls or new socks. My wonderful parents gave me the opportunity to compete with the best and get the experience I needed to be successful.

Nancy Lopez

A Drive in the Country

Golf is a game in which you try to put a small ball in a small hole with implements singularly unsuited to the purpose.

Winston Churchill

For years I listened to his golf stories, well, not so much stories as blow-by-blow accounts of every tee shot, fairway, rough, and hole he ever encountered. Then we came to an agreement: I wouldn't complain about the amount of golf he played if he didn't talk about the game afterward. Deal.

However, on a visit to our son and his wife in Colorado, I "did" eighteen holes and feel driven to share the experience, just this once.

The three of them—son, daughter-in-law, and husband—were off to play a round of golf and "Would I join them" just to enjoy the scenery and fresh air, since there was a spare seat in one of the carts? So OK, I decided I shouldn't knock it until I tried it. Not the golf you understand, just the fresh air and scenery bit. It's Colorado, high in the Rockies, on a very swish golf course—what could be bad?

Hole 1. The beautiful vista of the golf course was laid out below us, lush and green with aspens shimmering gently in every whisper of the wind.

After a few whacks they finally got their little balls in hole number one.

Hole 2. A strange creature sat on his haunches watching us. Jenny told me it was called a whistling pig. It was cute.

They lose one ball and pot the other two.

Hole 3. We passed several beautiful homes and saw another whistling pig.

Three balls, ten hits, one miss, and we're done, on to the next hole.

Hole 4. I was getting a little bored, but the sight of a group of sweet little chipmunks, and a hospitality cart, cheered me up.

One gin and tonic, about twelve hits, three "sinkings," and we're off to five.

Hole 5. We drove beside a crystal-clear river. I was suddenly aware that there seemed to be no bathrooms out here.

I forgot to watch the golfers.

Hole 6. Passed a house where three people were soaking in a hot tub; I pretend to concentrate on the golfers.

They agonized over their choice of clubs and hit the dimpled demons, which landed and buried themselves in sand.

Hole 7. A bathroom! And the hospitality cart was here again, driven by a charming young lady named Cindy. She was studying political science at Colorado State College and golf in her spare time. I ordered another G and T, wished her a safe journey, and looked forward to seeing her again soon.

Hole 8. More whistling pigs and chipmunks, which were joined by crickets, buzzing insects, and flies. I was bitten by a deerfly.

Someone lost a ball in the rough, and when I went to help find it they warned me to watch out for the snakes! What was I doing out there?

Hole 9. We had to wait for a few minutes for the people in front. I was told we caught up with them because we only had three golfers and one handicap. I think they were referring to me. I sipped my G and T and ignored them.

My companions took the little woolen hats off their clubs and have at it again.

Hole 10. More of those oversized, furry rats! And what were they staring at anyway? There seemed to be a lot of mumbling about lack of birdies and bad lies and other talk obviously not aimed at me. I thought there were lots of birdies around and I was certainly not in the habit of lying, bad or otherwise!

Hole 11. I might have mentioned the wildflowers before, but it seemed like a good time to pick a few. The others muttered about things like doglegs, wedges, greenies, and chips. It sounded like a disgusting meal to me.

Hole 12. I tucked my wildflowers into the melted ice water in my drink cup, arranged them artistically and putting this makeshift vase into the cup holder. It cheered up the cart quite a bit. All we needed were a few cushions and a small rug.

They put the little hats back on their woods and we were off again.

Hole 13. My good friend Cindy appeared over the horizon. I think I was becoming a valued customer. We had a little chat about her boyfriend, Craig, and an upcoming trip to Cancun.

My companion golfers were standing around our cart, looking a little impatient, so we set off in search of yet another flag, just like all the others, and a hole, just like all the others.

Hole 14. A little late I noticed a sign stuck on the front of the cart that read: "Warning: Rollover and Falling Off may cause Death." I hung on with more care.

They were still chasing their dreams and inoffensive little white balls, which were getting more abuse than a losing baseball team.

Hole 15. My companions and I got teed off in our own distinctive ways. I heard a house phone ring. I seriously considered going in and taking a message; I couldn't bear an unanswered phone. I was persuaded to let it ring and told, like a small child, that we were nearly there.

Hole 16. Just two more holes to go. I offered to rake a bunker. There is an art to bunker raking, and I am not an artist. No matter which way I did it, I seemed to leave my footprints somewhere. I climbed back into the cart and sulked.

Hole 17. Seemed to have had a little nap, missed this hole entirely. Hope I didn't miss my best friend Cindy.

Hole 18. This was it, the last hole. I looked for the vanity mirror. I wanted to look my best when we returned to civilization. No vanity mirror. What kind of a vehicle was this anyway?

It was over. We parked the carts and, clutching my wilted flowers like a hippie's bridal bouquet, I trailed behind them to the car.

When one of them suggested the nineteenth hole, I blanched. There was more? But as it happens, I needn't have worried; it turned out to be my favorite.

So, just this once, I feel compelled to share my hole by hole account. I wonder what it is about golf that promotes such revelation, but I feel better having shared it.

Maybe next time my husband wants to discuss his round of golf, I might give it a closer listen.

Ann O'Farrell

Mother's Family Day Golf Outing

There's no question that golf is an all-family game. When our children were younger, my husband and I used to take the two of them out to our golf club for a family togetherness day for eighteen holes if neither child started whining about blisters, stepping in goose poop, and/or the cheap balls that their parents made them play with that didn't land where they were supposed to because they were cheap. Eighteen holes if the father, he of the terrible temper, was able to keep in mind that some kind of an example, preferably good, for the boy child and the girl child, was the purpose of Family Togetherness Day. Eighteen holes if the mother was able to keep her intestines from turning into a knotted mass of pain because the father was not keeping in mind the purpose of Family Togetherness Day. (Knotted intestines were usually followed by a quick exodus from the golf course by the mother, often with one or both of the children.)

This was back in the days when mechanized golf carts weren't a must, and one could pull, carry, or drag one's clubs and count a round of golf as one's exercise for the day. The boy child and the girl child each had their own little bags, which, although not very heavy, always wound up on the backs of one or both of the parents. There was no hole that did not call for a family conference about which club to use. This, unfortunately, slowed things up quite a bit, which, in turn, called for allowing other club members to play through, which, of course, slowed things up even more.

The girl child had gotten her "golf basic" in camp. Having her "golf basic" meant that she was aware of the correct position of the hands on a golf club, the correct stance over a golf ball, and what golf outfit displayed her legs to best advantage. The boy child, the younger of the two, knew only that golf was a way in which to display all the strength he had in his entire seventy-eight-pound body and to hit that sucker as hard as he could, assuming (and hoping) that it would go . . . somewhere, because if it didn't leave the ground, his little arms would be vibrating for the rest of the day. The mission of the mother was to demonstrate good humor, good sportsmanship, and a strong sense of self-worth when laughed at, mocked, and/or scorned. She also was in charge of toting the bottle of something cold and liquid that by the end of the golf day had reached the temperature of a very sick baby.

At the first tee (really, at every tee) the father would take several—often more than several—practice swings before actually teeing up. This called for no practice swings by anybody else, anywhere. Also, absolute silence from all family members, meaning not only no coughing, no sneezing, and no complaining, but also no moving at all. None! And if the father's ball did not go in a straight line down the precise middle of the fairway, it was understood that someone had breathed too heavily or too long. The next to hit would be the children, during which a great deal of time was consumed by coaching from the father in a helpful manner, such as (to the girl child), "You're hitting a ball, honey, not ballet dancing," and (to the boy child), "You don't have to prove you're Attila the Hun, son . . . just try to get a little rhythm in that swing." Then, if the next foursome was not actually breathing down her neck, the mother would tee up, and if she managed to keep her eyes open, hook or slice, or if she had not managed to keep her eyes open, just pick up the ball and accompany her family to the next hole while whispering to the children that goodwill on their part would be followed by hamburgers, fried chicken, and all the frozen custard they could stuff down their throats.

Only once on these family togetherness days on the golf course did a near disastrous occurrence transpire. That was the time the boy child picked up an iron and, from about seventy yards off the tee, gave a mighty swing, causing the ball to rise to a majestic height and then, strangely, almost magically, disappear. It was searched for by all, but being nowhere to be found, it resulted in a discourse from the father about how rhythm rather than strength, a relaxed swing rather than a pushed one, was the secret of a decent golf game, and (wearily) why did it seem to be necessary to repeat this simple mantra so often? This query was not answered by anyone because, really, what could anyone have said anyway, until the girl child, having removed the flag for the father's putt, discovered the boy child's ball in the hole and foolishly announced the same, followed by a stunned silence during which nothing more could be heard than the chirping of a few birds and the buzz of many mosquitoes. At that, being aware that silence is often the better part of wisdom, mother and children rapidly faded away, each muttering something about needing to get some shade or to use the facilities, but aside from that single incident, the memories of togetherness on the golf course have gone down in our family album in the form of many nice sunny snapshots of parents and children, the latter even occasionally smiling.

Unlike the pictures of other sports, however (such as riding, tennis, swimming), which are dated and appended by clever captions improvised by the mother, the golf snapshots are accompanied by a dearth of comments.

Patricia Hentz Regensburg

"Mr. Johnson dressed his kids in some really spooky Halloween costumes . . . some of his old golf outfits."

Growing, Giggles, and Golf

Golf is like marbles for adults.

Source Unknown

The round of golf that will forever be remembered isn't necessarily the one with the lowest score, the one in a tropical paradise, or at a famous club. Sometimes it's the innocent interactions of people that bring the fondest memories. I can't help but smile when I recall a certain round of golf with my husband a few years ago.

Paired with two preteen boys, my husband Michael was a role model of golf etiquette—courteous, prompt, and emotionally controlled. As he demonstrated this fine gentlemanly behavior, he was also quite complimentary.

Overall the young men in our party were a refreshing change from the rowdy, boorish pairings that frequently occur at the public course. They were obviously not newcomers to the game and engaged in appropriate social interactions with a little encouragement, but every once in a while the bridge to manhood grew infinitely longer. The pair of wide-eyed faces grew red, and lips pressed tightly against teeth as they tried in vain to suppress an outburst of emotion—giggles.

Their embarrassment over losing control was evident. As the giggles began, they quickly turned from us and spewed giggles into their golf bags or at some unknown, interesting object on the adjacent fairway. This attempt to disguise their behavior was successful to some degree. Seriously preoccupied with his round and his attempts to mold these young players into respectable golfers, Michael did not notice.

At first I assumed there was something about us that brought out the laughter. We were four times their age; perhaps our wardrobe or lack of body piercing was the source. But by the third hole I noticed a definite pattern to their behavior. One of the boys would hit his ball or putt. Michael would provide the appropriate compliment, like, "Nice ball." A furtive glance at me, then the giggles would ensue.

Then it hit me: preteen boys had enhanced awareness of developing bodies and their respective functions. Every noun, every verb has a second meaning somehow related to the varying attributes of men and women. "Nice ball" may as well have been a quote from a girlie magazine. My feminine presence just added fuel to the fire. Michael had no idea what his innocent comments were doing to the formative psyche of our companions.

I wouldn't trade anything for having the best seat in the house for the comedic presentation that day. The interactions between these three males were priceless as the game continued.

"Nice hole." Giggle into the flagpin.

"Nice drive: long and straight." Giggle into your buddy's back.

"That ball may be wet." Giggle to the grass as you pretend to search for strays.

Michael topped himself at the ninth green, however. He gave the youngsters some used golf balls from his bag. "Here," he said. "You guys can play with my old balls."

Rachel S. Neal

The Challenge of Design

If the mind is full of fear or failure, a dread of the next approach, a persistent thought of three putts although the green is still far away, then, in my experience, there is but one thing that can at all help and that is to see the humor of the situation.

Joyce Wethered

Golf season approached.

My family, who were accomplished players on the fairway, had once again tried to convince me to venture onto the course.

"Golf is enjoyable."

"You don't have to be an expert to have a good time."

"Look at the benefits: exercise, fresh air, sunshine, and lunch afterward."

How could I refuse?

All that and being with family members conjured up visions of a delightful day for making memories.

Flattered by their coaxing, I gave in—I even went and

bought one of those cute little pink and white outfits with a matching visor.

If I am to play, I thought, *I have to appear not to be the novice I know I am.*

Once on the course, and even before I picked up a club, I did a few minutes of light stretching and took a few practice swings at an imaginary ball as instructed.

My three playing partners took their turns before me; all decent shots.

I marveled at how professionally they approached the game; I knew my skills weren't there, but I attempted to match their enthusiasm.

I teed up, addressed the ball, and fired away.

The first swing produced two immediate results: "all air"—no contact with the ball—embarrassment.

"Guess my best swing occurred during my practice session with that imaginary ball."

I giggled at my sense of humor. No one else did.

After a brief silence someone said, "Try it again."

I sighed, nodded, and repositioned myself. . . . head down, eye on ball, elbow straight . . . swing and contact.

The intimidating white ball actually moved a few inches from the tee, which to me meant success.

I smiled at the rest of my foursome and sheepishly said, "I hit it!"

And so it began.

Golf's disposition consists of being considered a gentleman's game with precise rules of etiquette, which I greatly admired.

But I now understand there's just so much patience and acceptance one can offer a severely "golf-challenged" novice, no matter their station in the family.

By the ninth hole, I sensed a nervous tension creeping

onto the scene, noticed the onset of the "meltdown syndrome," and felt terrible.

After having to hunt for *my ball*, which inevitably bounced off the course and disappeared, to retrieve *my ball* wedged between tree branches, to fish *my ball* out of the pond, or just having to stop to let others play through, how could I not take on the responsibility?

I somehow knew that if I were asked to join them again, it'd be to keep score, nothing more.

Yet I persevered.

I watched their precise form, marveled at their subtle techniques, and admired their skills.

I tried to analyze the game and the players, to get inside their heads to know what drove them to want to return as often as possible.

I tried to learn as much as I could to improve my game, all to no avail.

Maybe, I thought, *if that hole in one would make itself known to me, I'd surprise and delight my playing partners and create an everlasting memory.*

Stroke after stroke, I forged ahead.

Stroke after stroke, I thanked them for including me in their favorite pastime and sharing their expertise.

Stroke after stroke, I recognized this course's design, with all its obstacles, transcended my abilities and vowed never to return to *this* miniature golf course—unless requested to be part of this foursome again.

Helen C. Colella

"They won't go in the hole."

Daddy Caddy

Far away there in the sunshine are my highest aspirations. I may not reach them, but I can look up and see their beauty, believe in them, and try to follow where they lead.

Louisa May Alcott

Like so many female players, I credit my dad for sparking my interest in golf and encouraging me in the game.

When I was a kid, he and I golfed a lot. We went to the driving range to work on our swings. We spent time chipping, putting, and playing nine holes at the public course. We paired up for several father/daughter tournaments.

I took a lot of ribbing from my junior high school friends. They considered his breadth and brawn, took in his coffee-bean eyes, and widened their own at his accent.

"Uh, is your dad part of the Mafia?" they'd jest. "Is he out to get us?"

At six feet, three inches and a hefty 250 pounds, Pete Rizzo *is* impressive. Brooklyn born, my teddy bear of a dad is talkative (yes, even on the course) and a real type A personality. An Italian through and through, he puts family on a pedestal.

And, like most golf fanatics, he reads all the magazines and thinks he's a coach—my coach, my personal coach, *and* my caddy.

Now, that's a touchy combination under any circumstance.

It's common among younger golfers who are competing for small purses to use their dads as caddies to cut expenses. We take with us our biggest fans and our pickiest critics. They pick our shots, line up our putts, and remind us to concentrate. You might say it's the best—and worst—of both worlds. Especially in my case.

Although he thinks of himself as just one of the guys, Dad is an accident waiting to happen. And it inevitably happens during one of my tournaments.

Take the eighteenth hole at the state amateur competition, for example.

I was playing a good game when I turned to request a sand wedge, and gasped. Droplets of blood covered everything. They had splattered on my white golf bag, the irons . . . and my dad.

"What's going on?" I hissed in alarm. "What happened?"

"I smacked a mosquito," then came his steady response, "it must have gotten a vein." Sure enough, blood still squirted from his neck. He grabbed the towel and wrapped it around his collar line.

"Don't worry about me," he ordered. "Worry about your game."

Yeah, sure, Dad. But I tried.

Or what about my first year on the Futures Tour in Wisconsin?

As a newcomer to the league event, I was wired, tied for the lead, and going into the final three holes. We played to a huge gallery that rainy day.

"Please be careful, Dad," I tossed the cautionary words

casually over my shoulder. "The ground is getting slick."
Ka-boom!

Moving quickly in his excitement over my game, Dad
had slid on the grass, lost his balance, and rolled down the
hill. Ever the consummate caddy, he took my clubs with
him.

"Dad, Dad!" I raced to him. "Are you okay?"

He looked up from his soggy bed. "Don't worry about
me. Worry about your game."

Yeah, sure, Dad. I missed the green.

After several of his escapades, I started to get a lot of ribbing from my friends, who were always eager for the latest funny tale.

"Uh, is your dad out to get you?" they teased.

And then there was the final Futures event at York,
Pennsylvania.

Caddies were required, and my dad loves that rambling
course. Enough said. But by then, determined to appease,
he'd joined Weight Watchers and quit smoking in an effort
to get in shape and keep up with me.

I bogeyed the first hole and took a place on the shuttle.
Dad lifted my bag onto the cart and stood on the back. The
next thing I knew, he'd bounced off. We jerked to a stop.

"Dad!" I stood over him. "Can you get up?"

Not this time. He'd hit his head and possibly had a con-
cussion. He couldn't move. My fear was real and my tears
ran freely while we waited for the ambulance.

As they loaded him onto the gurney, he looked at me and
ordered, "Don't worry about me. Worry about your game."

I worried about both.

Although my mom went with him to the medical tent, I
was concerned about Dad's condition. Was the head
injury serious? Would he be okay? And I fretted over the
tournament. How could I play without the mandatory
caddy? Should I withdraw?

Although the caddy master arranged for a replacement caddy, I was crying and still rattled. I double-bogeyed the next hole. Then Dad returned to the course—walking on his own steam. I birdied seven of the last twelve holes and finished third. It was my best tournament of the year.

Even so, when he threw his arms around me in a congratulatory hug, I whispered firmly into his ear, "Consider yourself fired."

His black brows arched and his eyes twinkled as if to remind me, "Don't you still need a caddy next week?"

Yeah, sure, Dad.

Angie Rizzo

Funny Little Sport Called Golf

You're never too old to play golf. If you can walk you can play.

Louise Suggs

"Fore!" I shout as my club connects with the tiny ball, the tee, and the slightly wet grass. The tee and the ball slide a few feet ahead of me, to some unknown destination, but the chunk of soil beat them by two feet. I look down to where they all used to be, then at my father standing to my left. His hat shades the top half of his copper face, which only accentuates the smile that creeps across his skin. He shrugs just as a big laugh bursts from my mouth. He chuckles, still unsure of whether he should laugh. I offer a look of approval. This is why I play the game.

For years, I hated golf, but my father loved it. Every Saturday morning, he would awake as the sun announced its arrival, only to return as it rested. He even purchased glow-in-the-dark golf balls to prolong his game. It made no difference to him if Old Man Winter harassed his neck or the heat beat upon his head. The rain could force the other players away from the course, but as long as it remained open, my father was there.

If he was not playing the game, he was watching it, which is where my dislike was born. Never a big fan of any sport, the quiet game that consisted of older men with frumpy clothes, microscopic balls, and boring commentators tortured me before putting me to sleep. My father tried to explain the game to me, but I was not interested.

However, every Christmas since I was sixteen, he would take my mother and me to one of his favorite golf shops, some as far as a hundred miles away, so that we could buy him some bag, club, or gadget that would last him until the next year. He would look around for hours, practicing his swing or examining the newest balls or glove designs. My mother, who learned to love the game because she loved him, would offer suggestions to my father, which angered me because it meant we would be spending more time there. I would sulk in the corner while my father smiled like a child on his birthday, often glancing my way to show me the items that interested him.

Watching my father in a childish state, contrary to his everyday, hardworking demeanor, gradually began to please me, as did the stories that he frequently shared after his trips to the course. Once he told us a story about his best friend and golfing buddy being forced to jump out of the golf cart as they headed downhill toward a tree. My father laughed hysterically as he described how he guided the cart and himself to safety. That is when I realized that golf was more than a sport to my father. It was a time to relax, have fun, and bond. That is why he enjoyed my mother and me joining him to select his gift instead of giving him money.

When I bought a set of used clubs while he and I were out shopping on Saturday, a look of pride decorated his face, though he tried to hide it—just as he tries to cover his smile now. We do not get the opportunity to play often because we live in different states, but if we can make time during a family outing, we do. I still do not play well, although neither of us is in a hurry to improve my handicap. He has just as much fun teaching as I do learning, hitting more dirt than balls during the eighteen-hole journey. Now if *that* were a sport, I would definitely win. Playing golf is a means for my father and I to enjoy each other's company—heat, bunkers, and all.

Ashanti L. White

The Sixtieth Masters—A Gift to Gregory

I can honestly say that I was never affected by the question of the success of an undertaking. If I felt it was the right thing to do, I was for it regardless of the possible outcome.

Golda Meir

Gregory Norman, now eleven, first appeared at the Augusta National Golf Club before he was even born, when his mother strolled the grounds in Laura Ashley maternity dresses. This year, young Gregory was at home in Florida as his daddy climbed atop the leaderboard with a six-stroke lead heading into the final round of the 60th Masters Golf Tournament.

For the seventh time in his professional career, the elder Norman was heading into a major championship on Sunday with the lead, but only once before, in the 1986 British Open, had he won from that position. Majors vexed him.

Britain's Nick Faldo, two-time Masters green jacket winner, was in hot pursuit. Faldo closed the gap by five strokes, birdied all four of the par fives, and shot 67 for a

72-hole total of 276 and a victory.

What young Gregory Norman and the world watched, however, was more important, more exciting. Defeated, Daddy was gracious, honorable, and a true gentleman.

Airplanes, fancy cars, and a high-profile lifestyle do not make one bulletproof. There are no guarantees with this centuries-old game, of which the basic tenets are rules, manners, etiquette, and self-governance. In fact, the rulebook does not even start out with the rules; it begins with etiquette. No one is bigger than the game.

Gregory's daddy showed us all. Perhaps the elder Norman is like a modern-day Thomas Edison, who tried and failed thousands of times before finally inventing the lightbulb. Or Babe Ruth, who held the baseball record for the most home runs while also holding the record for the most strikeouts.

A champion also knows how to lose. Golf is the grandest game of all, but it is a sport. For centuries, though, it has been just a game and a mirror to life itself. It offers not only elation, but also despair on occasion.

From Greg Norman's desk, sent to him by a fan:

"Far better it is to dare mighty things, to win glorious triumphs, even though checkered by failure, than to rank with those poor souls who neither enjoy much nor suffer much because they live in the gray twilight that knows not victory nor defeat."—Teddy Roosevelt

Helen Casey

A Family Affair

What a wonderful life growing up on the golf course!

As a child I couldn't wait to go out to the course with Mom and Dad, but it wasn't to play the game. I liked to run around in the sand and roll down those beautiful green mounds that surrounded the greens of all eighteen holes. It was a weekly happening for my family some forty years ago, and I couldn't wait to get out there with them.

As the years went by, my playtime changed into joining them and actually playing the game. Before I knew it, I was hooked! I soon decided this was an addiction I couldn't kick, and after several years of encouragement from my mother, I decided to follow in her footsteps and join the Ladies Professional Golf Association (LPGA). She is now a Life Master Member and I am one and a half years away from becoming a Life Member. I am married to a wonderful man who is a member of the Professional Golf Association (PGA), and if it wasn't for golf, I don't think my family would have the relationship we have today.

Golf brought us together as one union and has given us a common bond for many years, and I know it will bring us many more years of joy and happiness. Golf has given us not only a lifetime of enjoyment, it has given us the opportunity to learn about each other's true personalities. We always have something to talk about at family gatherings, and we don't get bored sitting around looking for things to do, we just hop in our golf carts and jump on the first tee for a day of enjoying each other's company, hitting a few good shots, having some laughs at those missed shots, a little competition, and stories to exchange at the dinner table. Golf is a wonderful way for a family to grow, communicate, and stay united for an entire lifetime. I recommend it to any family that has the opportunity to spend a little quality time together!

Lisa D. Conley

The Cult

The reason the golf pro tells you to keep your head down is so you can't see him laughing.
                                                    Phyllis Diller

It's that time of year again. They are trying to recruit me. They want me to join their little cult and become one of them. I see the message in their eyes: "Resistance is futile." Perhaps they receive toaster ovens when they recruit enough drones for their khaki-clad army. They want me to pledge my allegiance to a teeny white god. They want me to be a golfer.

They start small. A television left on in the other room, announcers whispering monotonously about wind and grass and slopes. Soon, I don't even notice the voices. It is like they have become my own words. Someone asks who is leading, and I mindlessly rattle off the top players. *What? How did I know that? I am not even watching.* They smile in secret delight. They've tapped into my secret frequency and will now start manipulating my mind. It has begun within my own family. They emit sly utterances of which women golfers look hot in their new capris, or who is sporting which insignia upon their chest. They tap into my competitive nature by extolling the praises of the nine-months pregnant woman who completed the Ladies Professional Golf Association (LPGA) Tour that one summer. Now that's a tough woman, they say. *Yah,* I counter silently, *but I can just bet she had an epidural—unlike me. Who's the tough one now?* But the tiny spark of competition is growing.

They have charged my husband with my education as a golfer. He, who won the Alberta Junior Amateurs those many years ago. He, who has golfed at St. Andrews, with his rich Scottish heritage; golfing is in their blood like a virus. Before the commencement of my tutelage, I am full of anticipation. I am sure my lessons will entail biting my tongue and making deep, heavy sighs. In feverish dreams I recall the catastrophe of my first round, laughing during backswings and swatting at a mosquito during a putt. Who knew the level of silence required? These aren't athletes! They are supersensitive microphones, able to detect a fart from a fairways-length. They are motion detectors, calibrated to the batting of eyelashes. They have set their internal clocks at an unattainable pace. Forget the four-minute mile—who will be the first to set the seven-minute hole?

As the snow melts, they reach a new level of seduction. They want to turn my ambivalence into blind loyalty. They will give me just a taste. My husband, shrouded in innocence, offers to let me come to the driving range with him. Oops, he says, I accidentally got two buckets of balls, would you like to try? I am unaware of the sound of the hammer cocking. I lock my hands around the club and he explains the feeling of a coil. Coil up, uncoil. It's that easy. *Well, if it's that easy, I am sure I can do it.* The little white devil-ball trickles down the small slope and stops twenty feet away. I realize at the moment why the grass slopes gently away from me. It's pity. I glance down the line of golfers and wannabes like me. I spy a young boy who cranks the ball past the 150-yard sign. My neck stiffens and my teeth grit. I adjust my feet and feel instantly stupid as I realize I just "waggled." Again I look down the line and see others "waggling." The sound of a club slicing only air is deafening. I try another ball, and another. *Am I done with that bucket already?* Then I hit a ball, apparently, the right way. *How did I do that?* My body tries vainly to remember the movement deep in my muscles, so that I may reproduce it. The next few are, once again, duds.

My husband remains suspiciously silent. It must be killing him.

Once again, I balance myself and relax all the appropriate muscles. There it goes again! This time it is up in the air! *Uh oh, did I just woo-hoo?* I bring myself back to earth; they don't have me. *They won't snare me in their little sand trap. I'm stronger. I'll just hit a couple more balls, maybe another bucket.*

Heather Cook

I Am Living Proof
That This Game Makes No Sense

Children want to feel instinctively that their father is behind them as solid as a mountain, but, like a mountain, is something to look up to.

Dorothy Thompson

"I am living proof that this game makes no sense." That was my quote for the small-town newspaper and the country club after I hit a hole in one. I had played approximately twelve times in my life.

When people ask if I am a golfer, I emphatically say, "No." I am not a Golfer. I am a person who is occasionally found upon a golf course, chasing a little white ball around as if it held the meaning to life. I, however, know that it does not. Therefore, I am not a Golfer.

I really have no desire to ever be a Golfer. When I wake up on a beautiful summer day, I do not think to myself, *What a great day to go spend a lot of money to get ticked off and needlessly raise my blood pressure!* I prefer the solitude of hiking in the woods and appreciating nature without the fear of having my head whacked by a stray ball or the distant sounds of swearing.

So why, one might ask, do I play golf at all? In a word . . . Dad. My dear, wonderful dad is a Golfer. And so a few years ago, while visiting my parents for dinner, my dad walked over to the closet and pulled out two sets of beginner clubs, one each for my sister and I. Subtle, he's not. But I decided that if he's paying and he begs his "girls" (we are each in our early thirties) to spend some time with their "daddy" while doing the sport he loves, I can't really argue.

At first, there was hope. Within my first few trips to the driving range, my dad proudly exclaimed that I had a natural swing. I didn't hit far, but I hit straight . . . and every golfer I've ever talked to says that matters most. One of the first holes I ever played, I made par. I had mixed feelings; I didn't really know what I was doing, so how could I take any credit? But my dad was beaming with pride, and that was all that mattered.

So I decided that I could handle playing this game occasionally, as long as it makes Daddy happy (and he's paying). And besides, I'm good! I'm a natural!

That's when it all went downhill. The more I thought about the game, the worse I became. It reached the point that I had to walk the ball half the time, and in frustration I stayed in the cart and manned the Bloody Marys, muttering to myself that I should have stuck to my original feelings about the game—as in, not to play, EVER.

So I all but gave up the game before I really had even started. I only have played perhaps two or three times each summer for the last few years, whenever my parents succeed in dragging me along with them, which usually requires a bribe of a steak dinner following the game.

And so came that Fateful Day. We had road-tripped out to Wisconsin to attend my cousin's wedding, and the bride's father rented out the back nine at his country club in order to hold a family tournament. It was a shotgun start, and several holes had the typical prize-winning enticements; longest drive, longest putt, and, of course, closest to the pin, on hole thirteen.

As fate would have it, my sister, her husband, and I were paired up with a single guy around my age. As we drove our carts out to hole thirteen, our starting hole, I apologized to the poor unsuspecting soul in advance for my horrid playing. I had already felt the smothering gaze of several of the elder members of the club, all stereotypical "good ole boys" who clearly still believed that golf should have remained a sport that was only open to men. I prayed my partner wasn't one of them. It could, in that case, be a very long day.

"I really hope you're not one of those people who are serious about this game," I warned as I sipped from my third Bloody Mary of the morning. "I usually start out well, and then as I think about it, my game goes quickly downhill."

That is part of why I will never be a Golfer. I don't like apologizing for the fact that I'm bad; I despise the obligation of not only playing up to my own impossible standards, but also to the standards of others. I like sports where it's Me against Me. Not Me against my teammates, or Me against gender stereotypes. I always felt that unspoken pressure for women to not only play equally, but play better than the men. But, I could tell our fourth partner was going to be just our style: cool, fun, and relaxed.

We drove up to our first hole of the morning (and for the year, as I had not played since the previous summer). I went to my clubs and looked at my sister for guidance, and she told me what club she thought I should use. I don't even play enough to understand how you tell what club to use. Since she's stronger and a much better shot, I always up mine a bit. So I grabbed my three wood, and everyone laughed at me because it was only 147 yards. But today, I did not care.

I stepped up to the tee, and without warming up (and with only an obligatory glance to line up my shot), I hit the ball. Here's another clue as to how to tell I am not a Golfer—I can never follow the ball, EVER. And so, since the only people I play with are my family, it is an unwritten rule that everyone else follows my ball, and then tells me where to go after it has found its spot. So immediately after my shot, I walked away, since I knew my sister would be following my ball for me.

Suddenly I stopped talking long enough to listen to my partner, who was laughing in disbelief and saying, "It's in! It's in the hole!" while pointing toward the green.

Confused, I turned around to look at what in the world he was pointing at. I could see in the distance my sister and her husband on the green jumping up and down, high-fiving, and doing something close to jumping jacks.

"You got a hole in one! It's in! It's a hole in one!" I could hear them yelling.

I what? I said to myself. *There's no possible . . .* I felt a little flutter of anticipation, but more confusion and disbelief. My partner made me get in the cart and we drove down to the green. The greens keeper had motored over on his lawnmower, as he had witnessed the entire thing. My parents and aunt and uncle had been on the neighboring hole, and came running over when they heard all the yelling.

That, in essence, is how I made my "Hole in One that I Never Got to See." But the rest of the day, I didn't care how I played, and it was the most fun I had ever had. The only thing that dampened my elation was when my partner informed me that it is tradition for anyone who gets a hole in one to buy everyone else drinks.

"What?" I screeched in disbelief. "That's the single most

ridiculous thing I've ever heard of! I knew I didn't play this game for a reason!!"

Of all times to get a hole in one, this was the best. When else would I have my entire extended family there to celebrate with me? I was nearly at celebrity status; but I soon discovered that in the golf world, not everyone shares in your success. As I skipped, sauntered, and sashayed my way back to the pro shop, I did so under the smothering glares of the Good Ole' Boys contingency. In the midst of my happiness, they were more scowling, more mean-spirited, and more bitter than ever. Someone got a hole in one, and it wasn't one of them. It's a tourist, and a novice, and a WOMAN.

That's OK. I attained what most of them had spent every Sunday morning of their adult life trying to attain, on only my twelfth game ever. I guess that's what happens when you loosen up and just enjoy the game.

As my dad hugged me, pride beaming from his every pore, I asked him, "Now that I reached the greatest accomplishment of this sport, does that mean I don't have to play anymore?"

Stacy Smith

The Ace of Clubs

Children are not things to be molded, but are people to be unfolded.

Jess Lair

Golf is a selfish game.

It greedily commands your attention, your focus, and your time. It demands centering, commitment, and sacrifice. I understand that. But the payoff is huge in satisfaction alone.

Golf is also a giving game.

It shapes character, strengthens friendships, and bonds families. I know that. As a tomboy athlete, I was drawn to golf and achieved my ranking in the Ladies Professional Golf Association (LPGA), thanks to the early training from my dad and the ongoing support of my coach, my husband, and my friends.

When I insisted—at the tender age of five—on learning to play, my dad sawed down a club and gave it to me. He spent hours teaching and encouraging me. My mom, too, took me around the course with her. Perhaps that's why, when I was blessed with the birth of my son, Nicholas, it felt natural to tote him along.

In fact, the driving range was the destination of his first outing—at four days old. I propped his infant car seat in the stroller and he slept while I pulled out my wedge and practiced. At nine weeks, Nicholas boarded his first airplane; I took him to Florida so I could work with my coach. Nick accompanied me to the golf course nearly every day for the first year of his life. He cooed from the stroller and gurgled from the golf cart while I leisurely played and worked on my game.

When he started walking at eleven months, I handed him a plastic golf club. He did his best to knock some balls around the range. By sixteen months, he was swinging his own cut-down junior club and hitting balls with me— sporting the most natural little swing.

I let him inside the ropes with me during my practice sessions. His infectious laugh soared right along with his balls. Stocky and freckled, Nicholas drew every spectator's eye. They were more entertained watching him than me!

One summer day, we were at Desert Mountain golf club in Scottsdale. After an hour of chipping together, I ruffled his sun-warmed, shiny brown hair.

"It's time to go, honey."

"Not yet, Mom," my two-and-a-half-year-old begged. "I have to chip one in before I can leave." His green eyes flashed. "I want to be like Tiger Woods."

Now, I ask you, what pro-golfer mom could resist giving in to a desire like that?

Nick played and practiced a lot of golf. If it wasn't with me, it was with his grandpa, grandma, dad, or stepdad. He had lots of encouragement and oodles of support. He traveled with me to nearly every tournament. On the odd week off, we stayed in my native Ohio with my parents, where Nick was in heaven: his Pappa and Nan lived on the golf course, right beside the sixth green.

On a February day in 2002, I left the family in Arizona

while I was in Daytona Beach at the LPGA International filming a DSW commercial for my sponsor. During a break, my cell phone rang.

"Mom?" Nick's breathless voice greeted me. "Mom, you're not going to believe this."

"Believe what, honey?"

"I just flushed a seven iron and hit it in for a hole in one!" His voice rose in triumph.

Yeah, right, I thought. Aloud I said, "That's great honey. Now, can I speak to Pappa?"

My dad gave me the play-by-play.

"It was the second hole, Kristal," he confirmed, "right here at the Mesa Family Fun Center. Only fifty-five yards long, but Nick hit a nice high shot right at the hole and it took one bounce . . . then rolled right in."

Unbelievable!

And my little ace was a mere three years and thirty-seven days old. To that date, Nicholas was the youngest player ever to record a hole in one.

(For the record, *I* played golf for twenty-eight years before I recorded *my* first hole in one at age thirty-three.)

Golf is a family game. It instills excitement, passion, and pride. I understand that. I know that. After all, my family lives and breathes it . . . from one generation to the next.

Kristal Parker-Manzo

4

GOLF IS A BEAUTIFUL WALK

Theme: Inspiration

Do your best, one shot at a time, then move on. Remember that golf is just a game.

Nancy Lopez

No Handicap

Men forget everything; women remember everything. That's why men need instant replays in sports. They've already forgotten what happened.

Rita Rudner

I will never forget the moment I first met Patrice Cooper. It was in the fall of 1989 and I was playing golf at Hazeltine National after my senior year at the University of Minnesota. Walking down an adjacent fairway was Patrice, focused, stalking the shot ahead.

I already knew Pat's story. How, as a twenty-four-year-old, she had been diagnosed in 1978 with a soft tissue sarcoma on her arm. How the Mayo Clinic saved her limb and her life and gave her a second chance. How she seized this opportunity to take up golf seriously. How she became the Women's Club Champion at Hazeltine with an established United States Golf Association handicap of three. And how, in 1987, her cancer returned and the verdict was pronounced: amputation above the elbow.

By the time I met her, Patrice was thirty-five and back

on the golf course—well-adjusted to the prosthetic left arm that she helped design—and now down to a *one* handicap. She'd faced and accepted her loss and, determined to move forward, made the decision to focus on her possibilities rather than her disabilities.

That first day I watched her. I watched her walk down the fairway, carrying her own clubs. I watched her routine at each hole. Watched the process it took to clamp a club in her golf-specific prosthetic and play out a shot. And I recognized immediately that Pat was a remarkable woman, a woman with commitment and passion for a game that sometimes eluded me. A woman I wanted to know.

Our friendship grew slowly through the years. We bumped into each other at golf events, met for dinner, and played a few rounds. I even used Pat and her daughter Nicole's home in Florida to prepare for the Ladies Professional Golf Association (LPGA) season. We drank a lot of wine, ate good food, and talked about everything from spirituality to the Minnesota Vikings.

And we played a lot of golf. We always played for money on a par-three hole. If you made a birdie on a par three, everyone in the group paid up: the Two Club. Pat and I called it a "two-dollar two." No matter how her game was that day, Pat could pull out a two at any time. I lost more money to her on the golf course than I ever won from her.

I admired her unsinkable will and indomitable spirit. When reporters asked if she ever threw a club in disgust or anger, Pat quipped, "No. By the time I unclamp it from my prosthesis, I've already calmed down!"

Pat caddied for me on the LPGA Tour several times. One steamy day in Augusta, Georgia, we left the practice range for the green. I stuck my Titleist glove around the handle of my black bag rather than in my pocket like I usually did.

We were the first to tee off, and when the announcer called my name, I reached in my pocket for my glove. When I realized it wasn't there, I turned to my caddy.

But she was staring down the fairway, absently using her teeth to tug my glove on her own hand and prepare for the drive. Pat was so intensely focused that she forgot she wasn't the one playing!

A seven-time Hazeltine club champion (six of those with one arm), Patrice managed to lure the National Amputee Golf Championship to her home club in 2003. As chairperson for the event—and an eleven-time champion in the National Amputee Golf Association (NAGA) women's division—she threw herself into the preparations. She was passionate about the event and the public opportunity it afforded amputees to pit their skills against other competitive players.

But it was then, after a sixteen-year hiatus, that Pat's cancer reared its ugly head once again. And both of us knew it was time to make the most of every moment.

Now it was my turn to caddy for Pat. I accompanied her to the amputee tournament that September. As host of the event, she didn't plan to participate. She had gone through two rounds of chemo and hadn't played golf in nearly four months, but her strong, competitive spirit insisted she give it a try.

Pat stood poised at the first tee. With close friends and family looking on, she hit a perfect draw down the middle of the fairway. She played three full rounds on two difficult courses. By the last hole, rain splattered down and umbrellas blossomed. But Patrice took her time and, true to form, calmly rolled in a twelve-foot putt to save par.

It was the last putt she ever made.

Without a second thought, I took a year's leave of absence from my spot on the LPGA Tour to serve as her caddy again—this time *off* the course. I drove her to radiation treatments three times a week. I supported her through two substantive and aggressive surgeries. I commiserated over the rods in her vertebra, the braces on her chest and neck, and the "halo" pinned to her skull. And, through it all, I felt privileged to assist in her caregiving, bring a bit of joy to her days . . . and help her segue gracefully through the end of her life.

Eleven brutal months after that last putt, Pat died. She was fifty-one.

Over the years, we had walked the course hundreds of times and I always knew that she was the one with the more impressive game. I never tired of admiring her smooth swing. I never tired of hearing her teasingly needle a partner. I never tired of helping her work out a new adjustment to her prosthetic. Through it all, the word "handicap" was never in her vocabulary. Her attitude was charming, her humor frank and . . . disarming.

Pat found delightful freedom in a game that manages to challenge and frustrate even the most whole-bodied players. Golf fed her passion. Golf gave her pleasure. More importantly, golf promised her possibilities.

Karen Weiss

Golf Legend's Drive Scores a Legacy

Doctors use various analogies when describing tumors. I'm sure you've heard someone say, "It was the size of a grapefruit!" or, "It was like a football!" I have a friend with an ovarian mass that was described as something akin to a bunch of bananas. It's no longer surprising when lumps are described as peas, walnuts, oranges, plums, avocados, baseballs, and . . . golf balls.

One woman's drive to make a difference, fueled by the trauma of losing a close friend and fellow golfer to breast cancer, and her intimate knowledge of the game surrounding these diminutive, dimpled, white orbs have created the recipe for a unique legacy that has raised more than $3.5 million (and counting) for breast cancer awareness, education, and research.

The impetus behind this fund-raising machine is Val Skinner, six-time Ladies Professional Golf Association (LPGA) winner, CBS and Golf Channel analyst, and tireless evangelist in her mission to prevent and ultimately cure this devastating disease. The Val Skinner Foundation hosts a one-day golf event—the LIFE Event—that generates a donation of $500,000 each year to advance breast cancer awareness, education, and research that will one

READER/CUSTOMER CARE SURVEY

We care about your opinions! Please take a moment to fill out our online Reader Survey at **http://survey.hcibooks.com**. As a **"THANK YOU"** you will receive a **VALUABLE INSTANT COUPON** towards future book purchases as well as a **SPECIAL GIFT** available only online! Or, you may mail this card back to us and we will send you a copy of our exciting catalog with your valuable coupon inside.

(PLEASE PRINT IN ALL CAPS)

First Name		M.I.	Last Name	

Address					Email		

State			Zip		City		

1. Gender
- ☐ Female ☐ Male

2. Age
- ☐ 8 or younger
- ☐ 9-12 ☐ 13-16
- ☐ 17-20 ☐ 21-30
- ☐ 31+

3. Did you receive this book as a gift?
- ☐ Yes ☐ No

4. Annual Household Income
- ☐ under $25,000
- ☐ $25,000 - $34,999
- ☐ $35,000 - $49,999
- ☐ $50,000 - $74,999
- ☐ over $75,000

5. What are the ages of the children living in your house?
- ☐ 0 - 14 ☐ 15+

6. Marital Status
- ☐ Single
- ☐ Married
- ☐ Divorced
- ☐ Widowed

7. How did you find out about the book?
(please choose one)
- ☐ Recommendation
- ☐ Store Display
- ☐ Online
- ☐ Catalog/Mailing
- ☐ Interview/Review

8. Where do you usually buy books?
(please choose one)
- ☐ Bookstore
- ☐ Online
- ☐ Book Club/Mail Order
- ☐ Price Club (Sam's Club, Costco's, etc.)
- ☐ Retail Store (Target, Wal-Mart, etc.)

9. What subject do you enjoy reading about the most?
(please choose one)
- ☐ Parenting/Family
- ☐ Relationships
- ☐ Recovery/Addictions
- ☐ Health/Nutrition
- ☐ Christianity
- ☐ Spirituality/Inspiration
- ☐ Business Self-help
- ☐ Women's Issues
- ☐ Sports

10. What attracts you most to a book?
(please choose one)
- ☐ Title
- ☐ Cover Design
- ☐ Author
- ☐ Content

TAPE IN MIDDLE; DO NOT STAPLE

BUSINESS REPLY MAIL
FIRST-CLASS MAIL PERMIT NO 45 DEERFIELD BEACH, FL

POSTAGE WILL BE PAID BY ADDRESSEE

Chicken Soup for the Soul®
3201 SW 15th Street
Deerfield Beach FL 33442-9875

FOLD HERE

Do you have your own Chicken Soup story
that you would like to send us?
Please submit at: **www.chickensoup.com**

Comments

day spare others from the heartache she experienced when her dear friend died at the age of twenty-eight.

Philanthropic corporate executives pay handsomely for the privilege of getting a few inside tips from the nationally ranked LPGA pros who generously give up their time year after year to make this event a consistent success. After all, how often is the casual golfer able to exercise bragging rights and share an anecdote or two about the last time he played golf with Nancy Lopez, Juli Inkster, or Karrie Webb?

The research that is funded by the LIFE Event is geared toward figuring out why and how the breast cancer that attacks and kills young women tends to be more aggressive. Some women are struck in their twenties and early thirties, the prime of their lives. Funds raised by this event have financed a center that provides genetic testing for young women with a strong family history of the disease. These funds also backed an interactive mobile tour that takes the message of early detection on the road, into communities and to college campuses.

One woman with a heart as big as Texas, one little ball, the memory of a friendship that was abruptly cut short, and a little help from her friends. Val Skinner believed she could make a difference. She already has.

Ann Sheridan

Run the Race with Patience

Adventures don't begin until you get into the forest. That first step is an act of faith.

Mickey Hart

Tears stung my eyes as I choked down the lump in my throat. I wished with all my heart I could quit and forget the entire event. But there I was, in the middle of the golf course with nowhere to go except toward the next fairway.

The sun was warm—the golf course green and lush. The sky held a few fluffy white clouds in its sea of blue. It should have been a perfect day, but it was far from that— at least it seemed that way at the moment.

I'd waited several months to play in this golf tournament. Here I was playing a golf hole where my score should have been no more than a seven . . . two over par for me. I'd just registered a whopping fourteen. FOURTEEN!

Everything that could possibly go wrong had.

All had been well for a few shots—until I landed in a bunker trap in front of the green. After four shots of trying to hit my ball out of the sand, there seemed only one thing left to do. I swung my club mightily, preparing for a clean stroke, and whacked it clean out of there—and out of bounds on the opposite side of the green. Two more strokes for going out-of-bounds. The rest of the hole has faded from memory, but the sting of discomfort still remains. Writing a fourteen down on a scorecard is not a pretty picture.

My partner and I had just met at the beginning of the day. "That hole's over, forget it," she said softly.

"Easy for you to say," I muttered to myself. Yet something in the way she said it forced me to heed her advice. I sensed that this petite little lady with blond-gray hair, a weathered face, and a determined attitude probably had forgotten more of life's lessons than I had ever learned.

We played the next few holes in silence as I tried to recover from my humiliation and, worst of all, my self-pity.

Her next words are etched in my memory: "I've had five cancer surgeries. I'm thrilled to be here and consider myself very lucky. God gives us little trials so we can cope with the big ones."

Humbly, my attitude slowly changed. I really was lucky to be there. Today's golf game certainly was not a matter of life or death.

Later I recalled words from a Sunday sermon: "Run with patience the particular race that God has set before us."

The sand trap that day had exhausted my patience, yet, somehow, I'd been given the strength to recover and go on with the game.

Thank you, God, for sand traps and little trials.

Marilyn Jaskulke

Unbridled

There are dreamers and there are planners; the planners make their dreams come true.

Unknown

Before I was thirteen, horses were my passion. I competed in jumping and equitation and even took the New Jersey State Championship. Although I played golf on occasion with the junior set of clubs my parents gave me, all I really wanted to do was drive the cart—until I sat in front of the television set and watched the 1988 Women's Kemper Open in Hawaii.

The leaderboard was stacked with great players—Betsy King, Nancy Lopez, Beth Daniel—and I could hardly contain my excitement. The women were hitting unbelievable shots, and they were neck and neck coming down to the last hole. Par five, reachable. Nancy went for it in two, chunked it into the water . . . and Betsy King won. For the first time ever, I was hooked on golf.

And Betsy King was my new idol.

I loved how Betsy kept herself even and balanced as she played. She never got too excited; she never got upset. I listened as the commentators referred to her northeastern roots, her athletic interests, and the Purple Paladins of her alma mater, Furman University. Then and there, I decided I wanted to be in the Ladies Professional Golf Association (LPGA). I told my dad to sell my horse, and I began practicing every day.

Early on, I established a handicap. It was my goal to cut it in half each summer. Somewhat of a perfectionist, I leaped at the challenge of hitting certain shots and improving my game. After all, I wanted to be Betsy King.

When I saw that she had a Ben Hogan fifty-six-degree sand wedge—the Hogan Special—I copped the identical one from my dad's golf bag.

She'd played basketball; I played basketball.

She wore Izod; I wore only Izod.

When I began winning junior tournaments, I researched golf camps and picked the one at Furman for three summers straight. I met the coach and worked hard so he would remember me when it came time to recruit.

And he did. I followed Betsy straight to Furman University in South Carolina. She had graduated in 1977; I would graduate in 1997.

In the spring of my freshman year, the coach brought Betsy in to motivate and inspire us. Little did he know.

After college, I turned professional. On a rookie tour in Dayton, Ohio, I was thrilled to be paired with Hall of Famers Beth Daniel and my secret idol, Betsy King. What an honor to play with two other Furman grads. But nervous and self-conscious in Betsy's presence, I doubled the first hole . . . a comedy of errors from the tee to the green.

In 2000, both Betsy and I appeared at the du Maurier Classic in Quebec. Just prior, I'd had a bad week in St. Louis and told my caddy I needed to have more fun. He complied by supplying me with a new joke every day of the tour to lift my spirits and brighten my outlook. It worked.

At the Royal Ottawa Golf Club, I stepped on every tee knowing I could make birdie. At the fifteenth hole, I made a good drive down the middle, but a poor second shot cost me a stroke. It took a thirty-footer to save par. That day, I made every putt I looked at—with twenty-three putts in all. In spite of contending with rain delays, winds, and unpredictable greens, it was my career-best round. I shot a five-under-par sixty-seven in the first round of the LPGA's final major championship of the year.

I floated into the media tent afterward where I flirted shamelessly with the reporters. They supplied endless questions and I answered, nearly giddy with my moment in the spotlight, in no rush to leave.

So when they asked about my inspiration, I expounded—at length—on Betsy King, her influence in my life, and our "commonalities."

Who knew those same reporters would interview Betsy later that day and tell her what I'd said? The newspapers related that she was "flattered" . . . somewhat . . . but said it made her feel old to have someone following her "since they were a kid."

After the tournament, still glowing, I found myself sitting in the airport across from Betsy King. We sat in mutual silence.

Without thinking, I spoke to cover my awkwardness. "Uh, I hear you're feeling old . . ."

"Good tournament," she offered, still even, still balanced.

Ah, Betsy King, still my idol.

Diana D'Alessio

On the Spot

I think the key is for women not to set any limits.

Martina Navratilova

I've never taken my career for granted. I felt blessed to be consistently in the top ten. But in the early 1980s, I encountered hazards of a different sort. I was experiencing back problems and sensed that my game was suffering, too. It wasn't long before negative thoughts seeped in, and I felt less in control. I feared I'd lost my momentum. In turn, this affected other things about me, and I began to question myself.

Finally, in 1983, I decided I needed a break and leased a place along the eastern seacoast of New Hampshire. For six months, I kicked back at my retreat. With plenty of time on my hands, I devoured books, entertained friends and family, and pursued one of my special interests— wine collecting. It was a valuable time to relax, rethink, and regroup, and I made the most of it.

I took long, solitary walks, my mind often as tumultuous as the waves pounding the beach. Did I still have something to offer the Ladies Professional Golf Association

(LPGA)? Did golf still have something to offer me? Was there more? Maybe I should call it quits. Maybe I should leave the game and move on with my life. I wrestled with my thoughts.

In the midst of all this introspection, I realized something important: there was nothing I needed to prove to myself or others, nothing at all. Furthermore, I appreciated that—unlike other sports—no one in golf tells you when to leave. You can play as long as you're eligible, and you can retire when the time is right for you. And, deep inside, I understood that, instinctively, when the time was right for *me* I would know.

Those simple thoughts revitalized me.

So, with my spirit and back healed at last, I decided to rededicate and rebrand myself. I sought out a new teacher. I changed equipment. And it wasn't long before I recognized that my finishes were getting stronger and I was on a firm, upward spiral.

In 1985, I qualified for the Mazda Japan Classic.

The tournament itself was elegant and ceremonious. A real fairy-tale place, the course was exquisite, beautiful, and serene. I felt privileged to compete there. But it was also a challenging and difficult layout. By the last day, I was only a few shots off the lead. I approached the greens with confidence and played as perfect a game as I'd ever played.

I shot a mind-dazzling sixty-four . . . and won!

I was nearly as elated with the Mazda RX7 they awarded me as I was with the victory. At the same time, I paused in amazement as I quite *physically* felt the urgent drive and passion to compete—which had driven me for so long—seep out of my body. Still in tune with myself more than a year after my "interval of introspection," I knew instantly that it was my personal signal to leave the game.

The time was right.

I might have second-guessed that thought. I might have wondered if I had more to give to golf. I might have questioned myself. But I didn't. I simply . . . knew. I knew it like I knew the sweet spot on my driver. I just knew.

And, I ask you, when better than then?

After a fifteen-year career high, I was at my peak, in the headlines, and the toast of the LPGA. So, in the span of one deep, long breath, I made the decision along with the announcement.

I would retire.

Even today, I feel fortunate that I made the choice when I did, and that I had the courage to celebrate success while turning my face to the future. Professional golf brought great joy and opportunity into my life, giving more than it took. It taught me lessons, introduced me to new friendships, and forged my character. I'll always consider it a wonderful, marvelous gift, a gift with a storybook ending.

Jane Blalock

Mind Matters

A long-standing convention states that 95 percent of a shot is determined in the mind. Physical strength, so they say, is only a small component. Agility and skill, mental toughness, course management, and equipment make up the remaining aspects of the game.

Perhaps that's why Gary Player once claimed that the next barrier in golf would be the mind. Well, I intended to break that barrier. After all, someone broke the "impossible" four-minute mile—and I was equally determined to do the impossible in golf. As an athlete, I desired to push myself as far as I could go. And I headed full force toward achieving that goal.

Following my formative years as an amateur in Canada, then as an alumnus of the University of Oklahoma, I became a medalist in 2003 at the Ladies Professional Golf Association (LPGA) Qualifying School. And I was the first woman in history to participate in the Professional Golf Association Tour's Q-School in California. Little did I know that, at only twenty-five, my health had already begun to deteriorate.

When chronic fatigue first plagued my days, I pointed at the rigors of travel and the demands of being a professional golfer. When nausea occurred, I suspected a virus—then invested in home pregnancy tests. When sleeplessness persisted, I blamed stress and an overactive mind. Even so, I was baffled. But when rapid heart rate and muscle weakness evidenced themselves, I really grew concerned.

My fine motor control dissolved. My concentration shattered. My strength waned. I took days off because, quite simply, I just felt sick. Anxiety, highly charged mood swings, and depression set in, putting a tremendous strain on all my relationships. I felt horrible and played even worse than I felt.

Although I trained as hard as ever, the work didn't pay off like I thought it should. My driving distance dropped—particularly shocking because I'm known for my athletic swing. Frustrated by not reaching the same spots on the courses as prior years, I trained even longer. I trained harder . . . and I grew weaker.

Hand and leg tremors, in conjunction with eye problems—difficulty with depth perception and alignment—caused me to overshoot. Once, I overshot the hole six times from three feet away on a flat surface. After a promising rookie year, I struggled in 2005, making just two cuts in nineteen events.

If shots truly were determined by the mind, then there was no hope. I thought I was losing mine!

Concerned at my racing pulse—130 beats per minute—my doctor ordered an electrocardiogram. Then he insisted on further tests, scans, and blood work. In November of 2005, my endocrinologist announced the diagnosis: I suffered from Grave's disease, an autoimmune disorder.

I finally had a reason for my long list of debilitating symptoms. And I discovered that all my extra training actually had increased muscle loss, especially bad news for an athlete.

Relieved to finally understand why my performances had crumbled over the last year, I still feared this chronic—and progressive—hyperthyroidism. Not only was my health under attack, but so were my dreams, desires, and hopes. Shattered, uncertainty and doubt clouded my thoughts.

Would I be able to face the reality of this challenge?

Would this insidious disease prevent me from playing golf again?

If I continued to play, would it affect my long-term game?

Over the next few months, I was ordered to stay home and rest—which necessitated my withdrawal from the LPGA Tour's Q-School. While my muscles atrophied even further, I took several medications to reduce my heart rate and my toxic thyroid hormone levels in preparation for further treatment. I decided to spend that time learning about Graves' disease. Confined to bed, I read books, spent hours searching the Internet, and interviewed other victims. But the more I investigated the ramifications of this treatable but incurable disease, the more I doubted, until Gail Devers returned an e-mail.

Diagnosed in 1990 with Graves, Gail went on to win the gold medal in the 100-meter dash at the 1992 Olympics. She selflessly talked me through my uncertainty. She discussed her comeback. She revealed how she beat the odds—by digging deep within to summon her spiritual and physical forces. Gail generously shared her inner strength as a fellow athlete and inspired me to hurdle this barrier in my own life.

Athlete to athlete, her insight encouraged me. Woman to woman, her words comforted me. Mind to mind, her perspective changed me. I listened. I believed.

For the first time, I felt a glimmer of hope.

After weighing my treatment choices, I opted for a total

thyroidectomy, or removal of the thyroid gland, and had a successful surgery in March 2006—thankfully with no complications. The surgery revealed that I have an additional autoimmune disease, Hashimoto's thyroiditis. But that knowledge doesn't daunt me now.

Like Gail, I've chosen to apply the skills I use in golf toward regaining my strength and my health. I'll train. I'll work out. I'll do the impossible.

Without a thyroid to wreak havoc on my body and emotions, I *will* adjust. With medication to control hormone levels, I *will* recover. With a positive attitude, I *will* grow from this hardship.

I'll push until only one barrier in golf remains: the mind. And I'll push past it, too.

Isabelle Beisiegel

A Range of Hope

"You only have six more months before your welfare benefits run out, you know," the social worker warned. Like I hadn't been marking off every day and every minute until it ran out. Like I didn't already know the light at the end of the tunnel was really an oncoming train.

"What are your plans?" the woman inquired, but with four young mouths to feed, no day care, and an ex who refused to pay decent child support, I didn't have any options.

I showed the social worker one of my hand-carved lawn ornaments. "I was thinking I could start my own business selling these," I ventured, but the social worker laughed.

"You can't run a business—you're on welfare!" she scoffed. I knew I'd succeed because I had no other choice.

What I didn't know was the dramatic turn my business plans would take or how bad things would get before my hard work and determination finally began to pay off.

It was two years ago that my husband walked out on me and our four children, Joseph, Christopher, Nicholas, and Shannon, then nine, six, four, and two. *What am I going to do?* I wondered that night as I sat at the kitchen table of my Massachusetts home tallying up the mortgage, car payment, utilities, and grocery bills. I barely had a dollar to my name. I didn't even have money for a lawyer, and my husband's attorney had advised him to pay only token child support until a judge ordered otherwise.

A stay-at-home mom, I had few job skills. And so I swallowed my pride and applied for public assistance and was turned down because my children had bank accounts.

"It's their birthday money, and it's only a few hundred dollars total," I protested, but rules were rules, so before I could receive any assistance I had to close the accounts.

When I returned to the welfare office I learned I was still ineligible because I drove a late-model minivan. It didn't matter that I couldn't make the payments, so I gave the title back to the bank.

With no car, an eviction notice from the mortgage company, and only a few boxes of spaghetti in the pantry, the welfare office finally granted me $370 every two weeks in emergency relief. But they also kept my child support checks to help pay for it.

By the time I got my first welfare check I spent most of it getting the power turned back on. The kids and I practically lived on hot dogs, pasta, and peanut butter. "Is this the best I can offer my family?" I cried myself to sleep at night.

The day the bankers stood on my front porch auctioning off our home I felt utterly humiliated. Luckily, an understanding landlord agreed to rent me a small house, despite my ruined credit—so at least we had a roof over our heads. But I couldn't afford school clothes for the kids. I couldn't even pay the registration fees so my boys could play soccer. So we found an old ball and played in the backyard, and on weekends we set up tents and pretended we were camping.

Other nights while the kids played Yahtzee I sat at the kitchen table carving tiny rabbits and frogs from blocks of pine. I sold my lawn ornaments for ten dollars apiece from a table in my front yard. Each ornament took several hours to carve, but often that ten dollars was the difference between having milk in the house or going without.

Because of new regulations, I could only stay on welfare for two years. By then I was expected to be employed, but for every minimum wage job I applied for, there were at least a dozen applicants as desperate as me to find work.

Maybe I can make a living selling my wood crafts, I thought, and began working even longer hours carving the tiny statues and building backpack racks like the one I'd made for our front hallway.

I asked the welfare department to send me to a business class to help me get started, but my social worker said it would be a waste of money. "You'd never succeed," she predicted, but I was determined to prove her wrong. I had to. My family was counting on me.

I knew that if I was going to do this, I'd have to do it on my own. And so in September 1999 I called Clark University, and they referred me to a new woman's enterprise center that offered a First Step Fast Track course for women who were thinking of starting their own businesses.

The center waived my tuition, and as I began attending night classes I also scouted out possible locations for my business. "That's perfect!" I exclaimed one afternoon when I spotted a small storefront alongside a dilapidated driving range. There was a "FOR RENT" sign on the building that looked like it'd been there for years.

Maybe the landlord will give me a break on the rent, I hoped as I dialed the number and introduced myself to the owner, Sam Kim.

Mr. Kim said he'd be happy to rent me the building, but there was a chance I might not be able to keep it long. "The store's part of the driving range, and I'm selling the whole business because I can't find anyone responsible to run it."

I didn't know the first thing about running a driving range. I couldn't remember the last time I'd even held a golf club. But I could hear opportunity knocking.

"What about me?" I blurted. "I could run it, and instead of a salary you could just pay me a share of the profits . . . if there are any."

Mr. Kim liked the idea, and a few days later we met to finalize the details. "Good luck," he wished, and as I stood staring at the overgrown grass and paint-peeling driving cages, I wondered: *What on earth have I gotten myself into?*

For my class project I researched the driving range business. I studied what equipment I would need and how much to charge, and I wrote up a feasibility study that was voted one of the best in the class.

This could really work, I thought, excited, but there was a major glitch in my plans. Because of weather I couldn't open the driving range until mid-March. But my benefits ran out in December, and the welfare office had denied my extension application.

I won't just be risking myself—I have four children to think about, I worried. But I worried even more what would become of us if I didn't take a chance and throw myself heart and soul into making this work.

And so from December to March the kids and I ate peanut butter sandwiches for breakfast, lunch, and dinner. I spent sixteen hours a day at the range cleaning and painting and getting ready for spring. And every night I prayed the utilities wouldn't get shut off again, or that the sheriff wouldn't show up with another eviction notice and leave us homeless.

By opening day I only had a few singles and some coins for the register. "Hope no one needs change," I told the kids. When the first customer handed me the exact amount, I considered it a sign from God.

We only had a few customers opening day, but the next

day there were a few more. At the end of the week, when Mr. Kim and I split the proceeds, there wasn't much, but I knew next week would be even better.

Sure enough, as word spread that the driving range was under new management, old customers began to return. "You've really fixed the place up nice," one man observed as he paid for his second jumbo basket of golf balls.

I spent every spare dime on new clubs, balls, and other supplies. But little by little my investments began to pay off, and by the end of the first season, business was booming. The second season was even better. Last year Mr. Kim offered to sell me the driving range, and he even helped out with financing.

Today, as my third season draws to a close, I can hold my head up high, knowing that I can support my family and I'll never have to rely on welfare again. Someday I hope to pass the business on to my children. Then they'll never have to worry where their next meal is coming from, either.

Now fifteen, Joseph often runs the driving range by himself, while my fiancé, Richard, and I spend time with our seven-month-old daughter, Cassandra. Christopher, Nicholas, and Shannon also earn spending money gathering golf balls and helping out at the new pro shop.

Sometimes I still can't believe how far the kids and I have come. "Mom, you really did it!" Nicholas said proudly one day as we filled baskets of golf balls.

"No I didn't," I said, pointing to the sign that reads ROYAL SPRINGS FAMILY GOLF CENTER. "We did it, all of us, together."

Heather Black
Originally appeared in *Women's World* magazine

The Inspirational Nancy Lopez

I am not consumed by the desire to play golf. Oh, I enjoy it enough when I get the opportunity; however, either due to choice or commitments, I have only played the game a half dozen times since the birth of my second child over six years ago. So it came as somewhat of a surprise when a friend of mine suggested I study the biography of golfer Nancy Lopez as an inspirational tonic for my hectic schedule.

"Biographies are like recipes for how to cope, how to succeed," advised my wise friend.

You see, I like self-help and inspirational books as much as the next no-time, overstressed, overburdened, and worn-out wife, mother, and soon-to-be-successful (I hope) entrepreneur. However, for me, I find even more fiber and substance in the biographical story of someone who had actually *done* it; they overcame the odds and the adversity. It is more than just theory, it is actual practice.

So I forged into the life story of Nancy Lopez, expecting to be regaled with stories of a childhood full of privilege and luxury. Of lazy summer days spent by the country club pool and afternoons strolling the manicured lawn called a golf course where some latent golfing talent would reveal itself in the form of a golfing prodigy. In the story of Nancy Lopez, I found my preconceived bias quickly dispelled.

Nancy Lopez was not born into a life of privilege. She was born in 1957 to a Mexican-American family of modest means. Nancy learned to golf from her father, Domingo. Domingo owned a local auto repair shop in Roswell, New Mexico, the town where Nancy grew up. He believed in his heart that his daughter would one day be famous, and he and his wife, Maria, scrimped and scraped together whatever they could to help their daughter succeed. He gave Nancy her first golf club, a sawed-off fairway wood, when she was eight years old. The family could not afford golf lessons, so Domingo was her teacher. Experts assert that Nancy Lopez has an unorthodox swing and maybe they are right. Then again, didn't they say the same thing about Arnold Palmer and Lee Trevino?

Perhaps Domingo did not give his daughter a picture-perfect golf swing, but he did give her a few gems that would prove to be like a suit of armor in the heat of competition. Domingo taught his daughter to "play happy." Even someone who has spent as little time on the golf course as I have can see the frown-etched faces of teenage golfers who wear a scowl like a badge of honor. At what point was it determined that if you do not spend half your day on the golf course lamenting your inadequacies, then you just were not trying hard enough? Are these the virtues we are instilling in our children? Not to Domingo. He taught Nancy that attitude was as important as technical performance and golf is a thinking-women's game. He would say the eventual winner is likely not the one with superior technical ability (in theory), but the one who has the mental fortitude to not tighten up under pressure. This is a powerful lesson whether one is putting for the win or trying to keep one's sanity in rush-hour traffic with a kid to pick up at soccer practice, or trying to fit a week's worth of work into a twenty-four-hour day.

Domingo also gave his daughter the right to believe in herself. He was so convinced of her abilities that he allowed his convictions and confidence to permeate his daughter's psyche. I found this to be another powerfully simple concept: to celebrate your child's unique strengths and gifts rather than constantly harping on their weaknesses.

Nancy Lopez soon began to deliver on the promise of her talents. At twelve years old, she won the New Mexico Amateur. As a teen, she won the United States Golf Association's Junior Girls Championship twice. At eighteen, she remarkably finished second in the U.S. Open. She led her high school golf team to two state titles. It should be mentioned that her high school golf team was otherwise comprised of all men. She went on to earn a college scholarship at Tulsa (the first woman to receive a full scholarship there) and in her freshman year she was an All-American and Tulsa's Female Athlete of the Year. Lopez turned professional at the end of her sophomore year in 1977.

Nancy had a strong start to her first professional season, but later that year, she lost her beloved mother after complications from surgery. As can be expected, the loss of her mother had a profound effect on her. But, with the heart of a champion, Nancy channeled her emotions with laser-like focus. She has called this time the turning point of her life and that which made her more mentally strong. In twenty-six tournaments in 1978, Nancy won nine times, including a stretch of five straight victories and a six-stroke win at the LPGA Championship. The next year, she repeated as the Player of the Year, in addition to another eight championships. Nancy continued her solid play until she had to cut back on her playing time in 1983 due to the birth of her first child. She ended up with three girls, and in 2002, she announced that she would no longer be maintaining a full playing schedule in order to spend more time with her family.

Nancy, who was inducted into the Hall of Fame at only thirty years old, ended her full-time playing career having won a total of forty-eight championships (she won her last tournament in 1997), and in 2000, she was recognized as one of the LPGA's top fifty players of all time. Through all of this success, Nancy continued to "play happy," infecting everyone with her warmth and charisma.

I know that life has a way of making us feel overwhelmed, but in the story of Nancy Lopez's life I found the inspiration I needed to not only tolerate life's challenges, but to tackle them head-on.

Donna Adams

5

UNFORGETTABLE MOMENTS

Theme: The Game's Ability to
Be a Vehicle for Transcendence

*You have to play the rules of golf just as you
have to live by the rules of life. There's no
other way.*

Babe Didrikson

Ms. Collette

She limped into the pro shop. I stood there, half in disbelief, half in amusement, shaking hands with my new student. Ms. Collette was my 3 PM lesson, showing up promptly at 2:45 with a new bag of golf clubs, plastic still on the club heads. She had to be nearing eighty years old, although I knew better than to ask a woman her age.

After the usual polite exchange, I got down to business. "Tell me about your golf game and what you hope to get out of today's lesson, Ms. Collette."

She explained to me that a well-known TV psychologist had said the other day, "If you want to meet a man then go where the men are." Ms. Collette was on the hunt and had decided that if men were on the golf course, that is where she should be too. She went on to explain that at the age of seventy-eight to be exact, she had been widowed ten years, and it was "time she moved on with her life." Ms. Collette had never taken a lesson, never hit a ball, never stepped foot on a golf course in her life. That was evident when she tiptoed on the putting green and asked, "Is this REAL grass?"

Ms. Collette and I met several times over the next three months. She showed great improvement, and I enjoyed introducing her to the game I loved. At one point, I was sure she was addicted to golf when I saw her hitting balls while fog and mist covered the range. She called out, "Practice AND a facial . . . how 'bout that?!"

Finally, the day came when Ms. Collette was ready to get out and play her first real nine-hole game. We played together, and she entertained me with stories from her childhood, from her first marriage, how she survived the tough times, and how she looked forward to a bright future and this new game. It was one of the most memorable times I have ever had on the course. I shot thirty-five and Ms. Collette shot fifty-six. It was a great start for her and a reminder to me that golf is a game we can enjoy on many levels. It does not matter how good a player you are. It's all about the companionship.

Speaking of companionship, six months later, Ms. Collette came into the pro shop, decked out in a new golf outfit. Her hair was fixed and just a touch of perfume filled the air. "I have a DATE!" she exclaimed. She was meeting a gentleman friend for nine holes and lunch. "If he can break fifty we'll go out again!"

One year later, I was on the dance floor at her wedding. Her new husband tapped me on the shoulder and took my hand. As we danced, he told me how grateful he was to me for introducing his new wife to his favorite game. He said, "It doesn't get any better than this. She's beautiful, she likes my cat, and she's a heck of a good sand player!"

They left the reception that day, walking under an array of seven irons, held up like the swords at military weddings. Golf had brought them together and would secure them through more than a decade of happiness together.

I last heard from them just a year ago, when Ms. Collette celebrated her ninetieth birthday. Included in the invitation was a picture of the gray-haired couple. Ms. Collette was holding a sign that said, "I beat my husband!" She had shot a 101, beating her husband by four strokes for the first time ever. She looked happy. They both did.

Anne Marie Goslak

". . . In sickness and in Golf."

A Mental Game

All is fair in love and golf.

American Proverb

Originally, it was my mom and dad's idea to play golf. They reserved Sunday afternoons for this family "bonding" experience, so we'd all head to the Moberly Country Club after morning church: my grandparents, aunt, uncle, cousins, sister, brother . . . all of us.

Surrounded by Missouri farmland, the nine-hole course backed up to wide fields of corn rows and soybean bushes. We played to a gallery of grazing horses and cud-chewing cows. The sun blazed. The humidity soared. Sweat trickled down the inside of my blouse as I lugged the bag from hole to hole, anticipating the only real incentive for this stupidity: a dip at the local swimming pool.

Yet, by the time I was fourteen, golf had seeped into my blood. In my heart, I knew I could be good. But I was your typical, miserable, belligerent teenager. I thought I knew everything, I didn't like much of anything, and I didn't want to be around anyone. In fact, I wanted to be somewhere else, anywhere else. And I tried to make everyone around me feel as wretched as I did.

Still, every Saturday morning I'd head to the course with my dad. And each time, I stared out the window and gave him the silent treatment all the way to the parking lot.

"I'll check in," said Dad as he walked toward the clubhouse. "Fine."

"You unload the clubs," he suggested.

"Fine." I dragged both bags to the first tee.

As always, Dad insisted I play first. "But you don't wanna tee off from the wussy tees, do you?" He arched his brows.

I stared through him and stomped back to the men's tee box. I perched a ball on its pedestal and addressed it. Feet positioned shoulder-wide, I flexed my suntanned knees and double-checked my grip. I gazed down the wooded hill where it flattened against the creek that edged the green.

Determined to prove myself, I drew back the driver, accelerating the club smoothly down and through the ball. *Crrrrrrack.*

The crack was as crisp and clean as the dawn that greeted us. The ball soared down the fairway, rising with a whoosh like a jet from a runway. I followed its whiteness against the perfect blue sky and emerald-bright grass. Suddenly, I knew that if I could paint, the club would be my brush and that picture would be my masterpiece.

"Not bad," Dad said, "for a girl."

I gritted my teeth. I knew I'd ripped it out there at least 180 yards. He made his drive: 230 yards.

My next shot was short of the green. Still, I bogeyed the hole. Dad made par.

"Nice chip, Dad," I grudgingly complimented. Secretly, I was pleased with my own play.

The second hole paralleled the first. Backing uphill

toward the parking lot, it doglegged to the left. There were two bunkers around the green to avoid. At 480 yards, it was a par five. It took me four to get onto the green and two putts to sink the ball. Another bogey. Dad made par.

"Pretty good," Dad nodded in satisfaction, "for a girl."

My eyes narrowed. My breath hissed through my teeth as I set my ball on the third tee. I'd show *him*. This time, I hit it harder—and my drive equaled his. I birdied the hole. Dad made par.

I whirled around and smirked. "So, Dad, don't you wish *you* could hit it like a girl?"

His proud grin stretched wide and he nodded toward our bags. "Let's see how you do on number four."

The rest of the round, our teasing was as smooth as our strokes. We discussed focus, stance, and mental game. Like always, he gave me pointers and I listened. Dad was in full teaching mode, and now I was receptive. Afterward, we grabbed drinks from the snack bar—an orange soda for me, a Diet Coke for Dad—and loaded our clubs into the trunk.

I buckled my seatbelt and Dad pulled out onto the highway. He drove. I looked out the window. And, once again, silence reigned.

But both of us knew, come next Saturday, we'd be out golfing together again.

Kristen Samp

G-O-L-F Is a Four-Letter Word

For as long as I can remember, the term "golf" was the worst four-letter word in my vocabulary. As a child, I came to associate the word "golf" with not having a father. Worse than a jealous mistress, golf had no respect for our family. The pastime consumed all of my father's attention. Weekends, Wednesday afternoons, and holidays would find him fleeing from our home, sporting a guilty countenance. I used to watch him as he loaded his prized collection of clubs into the trunk of our car. The head of each club was lovingly protected by a woolen cover, and I remember thinking that those clubs had more "socks" than my infant brother. His booties rarely matched, and were never as neatly attended to as those golf socks.

As I grew older, my father's obsession with the game became an accepted tradition in our home. If a school play were held on a Wednesday afternoon, I would know that only my mother would be applauding my performance. If a swimming competition were scheduled on a Saturday, I would know that only my mother would be cheering for our team. If a piano recital were scheduled on a Sunday afternoon, I would know only my mother would be subjected to my rendition of *Für Elise*. Other fathers drank beer, watched *Monday Night Football,* coached Little League; mine played golf.

As a teenager, my father's passion for the game began to irritate me. Those were the days of the early 1970s, before superstars like Tiger Woods transformed the game into a chic activity. During this time, I achieved a great deal of satisfaction by poking fun at middle-aged duffers. You know, those jelly-bellied "athletes" sporting pink shirts and green plaid pants, whiffing their weekends away. It was embarrassing. Images of Neanderthals grasping primitive clubs came to mind while I spent more civilized weekends reading, writing, and basking in the sun.

At the height of my derision, I felt the ultimate betrayal. My chief accomplice, namely my mother, embraced the game at age forty-five. Tired of being a so-called "golf widow," Mom took to the course in style, and within a short time, she had mastered the game enough to provide my father with a formidable opponent.

I, on the other hand, remained adamant. Let them make fools of themselves chasing a tiny ball down numerous fairways. I would have none of it.

As fate would have it, my relationship with the game of golf was about to change. Professionally, I had received a promotion to the director of fund-raising at a large urban hospital. Money was desperately needed to purchase cancer equipment, and the board of trustees had had their fill of vendor sales, art auctions, and black-tie dinners. What was needed was something different, something big, something exciting, and something expensive. I shuddered. I could feel it happening—an all-day golf outing was in the works, and I would be responsible for organizing it.

A week into my new job, my worst fear was confirmed. The hospital would sponsor "Links to Health—On Course to Conquer Cancer," with a goal of attracting 200 golfers and raising $200,000. I was doomed.

During our initial planning meetings, I was astounded at my ignorance of the game of golf. For example, while I knew the difference between a "hook" and a "slice," I had no knowledge of such phrases as "the Callaway system," "Big Berthas," "shotgun starts," and "mulligan sales." (When it was suggested to me that additional money could be raised by selling mulligans, I had originally thought we would need to apply for a temporary liquor license.) During this time, my *modus operandi* was simple. I kept my mouth shut, took copious notes, and read as much as I could about the dreaded four-letter word: golf.

A month before our outing, I decided to break the news to my father. I could only imagine his reaction. Me, his daughter, was organizing a golf outing! He'd never believe it. He'd probably keel over laughing. However, nothing could have been further from the truth. Upon hearing the news, he seemed rather awestruck, as if I were delivering some sort of beatific message. Then he asked, "What can I do to help?" and, "Do you have room for another foursome? I'd like to play."

Then I was baffled. I just didn't get it. I had graduated from college with honors, obtained a master's degree, secured a management position, married a wonderful man, owned my own home, yet, to my father, nothing seemed to compare to the fact that I was capable of organizing a golf outing.

Over the next four weeks, conversations between my father and me helped us gain a new level of respect for each other. In addition to discussing the upcoming outing, we talked about politics, the stock market, music, literature, and history. For the first time in my life, I felt as if I was discovering my father—and that dreaded four-letter word was responsible.

The day of the outing dawned rather ominous, with the prediction of thunderstorms. Tee-off time was scheduled at 1:00 PM, and by 12:50 PM, sunlight began streaming through the clouds. I like to think that a Higher Power played a role in that, knowing that all the proceeds from the event would be used to help cancer patients. The sunlight continued to hold until the last golfer completed the course. By the time we had gathered in the clubhouse to distribute "Big Berthas" to the winners, a fierce thunderstorm had rolled in.

When all was said and done, more than 200 golfers participated in the outing, and more than one hundred businesses supported our fund-raising journey. Our proceeds totaled an unprecedented $285,000. Six months later, the cancer equipment so desperately needed was purchased, providing hope to patients diagnosed with the disease.

To this day, I have yet to hold a golf club in my hand, but I view the game differently. Ironically, the very thing I despised most as a child brought me unqualified success as an adult both as a fund-raiser and as a daughter. Yes, "golf" is still a four-letter word, but so are the words "hope" and "love." And for me, I will forever associate the word "golf" with hope for cancer patients and love for a father.

Barbara Davey

AUTHOR'S NOTE: *Tired of sitting on the sidelines, I have recently taken a series of golf lessons, and I hope to be participating in the game this season with my seventy-five-year-old mother!*

The Rules Nazi

It was one of those weekly tournaments at our club. Checking the lineup of foursomes typed neatly on the pairings sheet in our locker room bulletin board, I saw HER name. Everyone knows who I'm talking about. Instead of settling down in her pillows with the *Da Vinci Code* or *Cosmo*, she's the person who goes to bed reading the *Rules of Golf*. You know, the one approved by R&A Rules Limited.

She knows every one—EVERY ONE—of the thirty-four rules and innumerable variations that are covered in more than 100 pages. She's the Ralph Nader of golf, the Martha Stewart of clean greens. I had never played with her before. She was new to the club and already she had a moniker: the "Rules Nazi." And if you could believe it, she was serious about her game: practiced before she played, took lessons, cleaned the grooves on her clubs. Terrifying.

"So you're playing with the Rules Nazi today," said Sue. "Sorry about that."

"Ever play with her?" I asked.

"Nope, but Ginny did last week and she was almost in tears."

"Why."

"She was disqualified for having sixteen clubs in her bag. The Rules Nazi counted them and called her on it."

"Not the end of the world."

"True."

"How did that happen?"

"Her husband had thrown a couple of extra clubs in her bag when he was cleaning the garage."

So here I was playing with the person who was already striking fear in the hearts of fellow players. On the second green, in one sweeping motion, with one hand, I replaced my ball and picked up my ball marker—one swift slight of hand.

"Unh un," SHE said. "I don't want to get sticky, but you can't do that." Her voice, I have to admit, was soft, sympathetic.

"Ey what?"

"You have to put your marker down first and then lift the ball. Then you have to place your ball back and then lift the marker."

"I thought that's what I did."

"No, you placed and lifted at the same time."

She was right of course. I checked later.

On the fifth hole, a par five went up the hill with a lot of trees and boulders on the left. Emily, another player in our foursome, hit her ball about eight feet into the woods with a boulder just in front.

"Want to take a provisional?" asked the Rules Nazi.

"Why?" asked Emily. (Just so you know, Emily spent HER evenings reading Danielle Steel.)

"Well, just in case you can't find it. Then you won't have to come back here and play another." (Rule #27-1).

"Oh, I'll find it," she said.

The Rules Nazi said nothing and off we went.

"I got it," shouted Emily happily. It was wedged in a root behind a tree. "I'm taking an unplayable lie," she said throwing her ball out of the woods onto the edge of the fairway, thereby exercising her perceived right (an often-abused rule) that by taking a one-stroke penalty, she could place her ball so that she got a clear shot of the green.

I wanted to say something. I was quite familiar with Rule #28, having been in that situation many times. But in this case, I was a coward, a wimp. Then (bless her) the Rules Nazi stepped in. "Sorry, Emily, but you can't do that."

"Can't do what? I'm taking the penalty."

"Well . . . you can drop the ball within two club lengths of where it is; you can take the shot over from where you first hit it but not nearer the hole; or you can drop it as far back as you want, but you've got to keep the place where it landed directly between the hole and the spot where you're dropping it. Sorry."

"Really," said Emily, "If I drop it back where you say I have to, I'll just be deeper in the woods. And two club lengths don't get me out of the trees either. So what you're saying is the only choice I have is to go back to the tee."

"Afraid so," said the Rules Nazi not unkindly.

I looked down at the ground sheepishly while Emily trudged back up the hill to the tee box. I could tell from the slope of her shoulders that she was not happy.

It was then that I realized I was in the state of huge cop-out. After all, we were playing in a tournament, and rules were rules. I found myself actually happy the Rules Nazi was keeping our game on a level playing field. Could be that the Rules Nazi wasn't so bad after all. And except for the rules lesson, she was easy. Even shared her trail mix with us, watched our drives, and helped us find our balls.

But you've got to wonder, *if you have to keep going to the Book or your club's designated Rules Nazi to play the game, can we call this fun?* Couldn't the rules be simplified for those of us who don't make our living playing golf? Hey, 250 years ago there were only thirty-four rules. Now there are 122 sections, 106 subsections, and more than 1,200 decisions trying to explain everything.

Makes you wonder whether you should even try to keep score.

Katharine Dyson

Save That Cart!

During a visit with their grammie, my nephews, Joshua, thirteen at the time, and his brother, Justin, eleven, joined their grandmother at Wood Haven for a game of golf. Vina had just been given a brand-new three-wheel pushcart, which held her still practically new golf clubs, her prescription eyeglasses, for which she had paid $650 and only worn once, and a small amount of money . . . $20.

Joshua was on one side of the large pond, starting off at the men's white tee. Vina and Justin were about forty to fifty yards from him, on the other side of the pond toward the left, starting off at the women's red tee.

In order to brace her cart, Vina wedged its front wheels into the stone steps leading to the tee box. She then placed her ball on the tee and began her first shot. In midswing, from the corner of her eye, she saw her cart begin to roll downhill toward the pond. Finishing her shot, she dropped the club and ran after her cart in an attempt to catch it before it hit the water. Unfortunately, she was too late. The cart rolled into the water and began to sink before Vina could get to it. Without even a thought for her own safety (did I mention she can't swim?), Vina went into the pond to rescue her cart and began dog-paddling toward the splash. Joshua, on the other side of the pond, knew his grammie could not swim and thought she was drowning . . . so he went running to her aid. Justin did the same, as both arrived just in time to help her retrieve the water-soaked cart and clubs and pull it onto dry ground. Everything was accounted for except for the twenty-dollar bill, which they saw floating a few feet out on the water. They made a mutual decision not to pursue any further rescue attempts and watched as the cash sunk to the depths of the pond.

Determined to let nothing dampen her spirits (pardon the pun) and prevent the continuance of her golf game, Vina decided to play on. As she sloshed in her shoes and dripped water from her clothing, she refused to be distracted. She noticed, on several occasions, that her two grandsons were snickering and whispering behind her but chose to ignore it. She realized they had probably never seen her with a hair out of place in their young lives. Not even her vanity was going to keep her from enjoying the rest of her day on the course.

In a short while the girl driving the beverage cart jumped out and ran over to her to inquire, "Ma'am . . . are you all right?" she asked.

"Well, yes, I am, though I did have a run-in with the pond on number six earlier," Vina answered. "Guess I look like a drowned rat, don't I?"

The girl began to laugh and both boys joined in her laughter until they could not laugh any longer. It was then the girl asked my sister, "Ma'am . . . would you like me to remove the moss that's hanging from your . . . uh . . . back-side . . . it is terribly . . . unbecoming!"

Christine Smith

Stamp of Approval

I've learned from experience that the greater part of our happiness or misery depends on our dispositions and not on our circumstances.

Martha Washington

During the lean years of my New Mexico childhood, Mother was as restrained with her S&H Green Stamps as she was with her words. She didn't spend either until it was necessary.

Every trip to the grocer and each tank of gas produced strips and sheets of the hoarded premiums. For my friends, licking and sticking the stamps into books—page by page—was a coveted assignment. But at my house, Mother kept track of the stamps, as determined as Scrooge to save and tally.

She was thrilled when she'd filled enough books to redeem them for an item of merchandise she'd longed for. Ever thrifty, Mother dreamed over the catalog, pondering the items and the best use of her stamps. Enough Green Stamps could mean tires for the Plymouth, stainless steel cookware for the kitchen, or an electric razor for Dad. Her decisions were thoughtful, decisive, and never willy-nilly.

"Kathrynne, how would you like to go to Odessa?" she asked one day.

My heart thumped with excitement. In the 1950s, the sixty-mile trip across the state line was always a full-day event. There would be customer orders to fill, the dress store to prowl, the shoe shop to explore. . . . We'd rest and people-watch at our favorite café. A burger, fries, and RC cola for me; Mother would order liver and onions.

"I think we should visit the Redemption Center," she added.

"Oh? What are you getting this time?"

"I thought we'd look at those Spalding golf clubs. See if you like them." Her coffee-bean eyes danced.

Spalding clubs? Professional clubs to replace the store-line brand Dad got through Whitworth Hardware? I drooled over them every time I peeked in the S&H catalog. Nearly sixteen years old, I was devoted to the game. It wasn't a passing fancy. My lessons, practice, and time on the greens proved that. And I understood that Mother's way of showing her support was by getting me the best she could afford.

Leaving Jal early the next morning, we headed south to Kermit, where we picked up the highway east toward Texas. Mesquite bushes, oil rigs, and cows dotted the flat expanse ahead of us, but in my mind I only saw golf clubs.

Mother downshifted when we approached Odessa and drove straight to the catalog store just off the main street.

There they were, practically standing at attention, a spiffy Spalding driver and a spanking new three wood. We eyed them on display.

"What do you think?" Mother asked. "Can you hit with them?"

"Oh, yesss," I breathed as I hefted first one and then the other. I placed my hands on the driver grip and considered how it set. Not that it mattered. "Yes," my tone of voice almost pleading, "these will do just fine."

Without another word, Mother approached the counter to finalize the deal. She and the clerk examined and counted the full pages of stamps. Then—without a hint of hesitancy—my frugal mother forked over her precious books.

I recognized both the sacrifice and the extravagance and loved her dearly for it. But she merely brushed aside my profuse thanks . . . and started saving stamps again. Licking and sticking to fill more books while I forged ahead with my golf and joined the Ladies Professional Golf Association (LPGA) Tour.

Over the next two decades, my folks caught as many of my tournaments as they could afford. But the most satisfying moment for me came in Houston, 1973. While Dad minded the store back home, Mother watched from the gallery and witnessed me win at the S&H Green Stamp Classic.

The irony wasn't lost on either of us. We flashed huge grins at each other during the awards presentation. I don't remember much about the trophy or the size of my winnings. But I vividly recall the premium they awarded me—ten thousand S&H Green Stamps!

I handed them immediately to Mother. At long last, I'd found the perfect way to show my true appreciation. I repaid her in full . . . and with interest.

Kathy Whitworth

Pastures to Greens

Golf is good for the soul. You get so mad at yourself you forget to hate your enemies.

Will Rogers

At age thirteen, I had a big crush on a little fella. A colt named Joker.

Of course, I loved his mother, Ribbon, too. I'd claimed her as my own the minute she was dropped off at our rural Oklahoma rental house. As a favor, Dad had agreed to tend her for a year during a coworker's absence. Neither knew at the time that she would be foaling. The guy never returned to get her.

I now had *two* horses. I was truly in horse heaven.

Although I'd never ridden before, I figured out how to saddle and bridle Ribbon. I planted my chubby, adolescent self on her back and spent hours and hours parading her around the pasture. Freckling in the summer sun, I repaired the fence to keep her in and, because there was no barn, built a crude lean-to against a couple of trees to protect her against the winter elements. And I took to riding my sorrel cow pony along the road, the train tracks, wherever I might find a few pop bottles to redeem for two cents apiece. Keeping a horse was costly. Dad expected me to feed her, and each bale of hay cost fifty cents.

When Joker was born, I tried to train him—more with love than any real skill.

"You can't get on the back of that horse," my dad warned. "He'll buck and throw you."

I bit back my concern and climbed on. But Joker was even more petrified than I was, and he took to me easily enough.

One day, I decided he was ready to leave the pasture. I mounted Ribbon and—with her reins in one hand and Joker's lead rope in the other—led him down a nearby bridle path that surrounded a public golf course.

Joker shied.

"Easy, boy," I soothed the skittish colt. "You're doing fine."

And then a train whistle blew.

Spooked, Joker jerked the rope from my hand and bolted—away from the approaching train, off the path, and right onto a fairway.

"Joker!" I yelled and urged Ribbon after the runaway. "Joker," I choked, scared I'd lost him.

Wild-eyed, the young horse galloped across the greens, hoofs gouging. Sobbing, I raced after him, divots flying. Startled, the grounds crew chased us, tractors roaring.

"Hey!" a man yelled. "You know better than to ride a horse in here!"

"We'll call the police!" someone threatened. "Get out!"

"This is gonna cost you!" another warned. "You'll pay for all this!"

The men finally cornered Joker in a stream and grabbed his rope. "You git on up to the clubhouse," they ordered. "The head pro will deal with you."

Still swiping at my tears, I smoothed the white blaze on

Ribbon's forehead while we waited at the clubhouse door. My heart raced. My hand trembled.

A slim, fit man walked out, paused, and gazed across the gashed greens. He watched me swallow a sob. "I've seen you somewhere before." His soft-spoken words surprised me.

"I . . . I came here awhile back to apply for a job."

His brow lifted.

"You . . . you said girls don't caddy." My eyes dropped to the sharp crease in his freshly pressed slacks.

"Why do you want a job?" he asked.

"To earn money." I looked him full in the face. "I need money to feed my horses."

Slowly, he adjusted his wire-rimmed glasses. "I tell you what. You teach my daughters how to ride a horse and we'll forget this ever happened."

No cops? No punishment? No restitution? I wasn't about to question the man or the bargain.

And so it began, my relationship with U. C. Ferguson . . . mild-mannered Fergie, golf pro.

Over the months, our families grew close. In return for my fulfilled obligations, he offered to teach me to golf.

I shied from the thought. "Hit a little white ball? When I could be riding horses?"

But Fergie invited me to the golf course one day. "I want you to see something."

"Can I ride over?"

"Yes. Tie him up behind the clubhouse," he said. "Oh, and Susie, leave Joker at home!"

That day, I stood back and observed Patty Berg teaching a golf clinic. Their bubbling laughter and obvious delight drew me like a horse to a sugar cube. Who knew golf was that much fun? Maybe I *would* try it out.

Now Fergie held the reins as, with love and skill, he introduced me to the game.

He gave me private lessons.

He showered me with friendship and favors, kindness and generosity.

He gave me my first set of clubs . . . used . . . with Patty Berg's name inscribed on them.

Fully hooked, I spent hours and hours at the course. Fergie encouraged me to approach the game with the same dogged determination I used to heft a heavy saddle or ride an untrained colt. I was, after all, in golf heaven.

Fergie mentored me through high school and expressed fatherly pride when I won the Oklahoma City Women's Amateur in 1959, 1960, and again in 1961. By the time I was eighteen, Fergie helped me land a golf scholarship to Oklahoma City University. He supported my decision to sell my beloved horses, so I could buy a car to get me there and launch my career in professional golf.

It was Fergie, soft-spoken golf pro, who took the lead rope and led this filly out of the pasture—and onto the greens.

Susie Maxwell Berning

Lateral Water Hazard

Why am I using a new putter? Because the last one didn't float so well.

Craig Stadler

My husband Jeff and I recently moved to a new home in Florida surrounded by a sprawling golf course. Jeff opted to retire in this community so he could play golf in his own backyard, nonstop, Sunday though Saturday. After two weeks of unpacking and arranging the furniture, he disappeared daily and I became a golfer's widow.

The new home meant everything to me, but the cluster of trees, bright-white sand bunkers, and the slopes of the golf course had captured my husband's heart. At sunup he'd cruise down the street in his newly purchased golf cart, making a break for that lush green course.

Golf is the game where grown men strike balls with clubs and trail after them on an emerald green playground. The game didn't interest me in the least. Only, I hadn't plan on breakfasting alone each morning when we retired. So I succumbed to the clubhouse schedule of playing cards, tennis, and exercising in the pool, but none of this nurtured my soul.

One clammy August morning my husband talked me into tagging along while he golfed. Then he convinced me to play. What a disaster! My white-knuckled grip on the club made my first stroke totally miss, the second sent a tuft of grass and mud flying, and the last one hurled the ball only a few yards. My hubby laughed at my debut, while my face slowly burned. Embarrassed, my competitive nature was bruised while my stomach churned.

In rebuttal, I drove to the library and selected a couple of golf instruction books. That's when I read that golf is a whole different ball game for women, the premise being that upper body strength separates the girls from the boys on the links. A week later, I made a daring decision to take the plunge and telephoned a golf instructor.

For six months I kept my secret smiling on the inside, until my instructor said, "It's time to play an actual game."

Few sports have so much equipment and nifty gadgets as golf. There's an essential range of wares designed to make you fashionable, comfortable, and more proficient on the fairways. I had fun shopping for gear and outfits, but would the clothes make the player? The next time my husband goaded me to play, I accepted, and he handed me the keys to the golf cart.

As instructed, I concentrated on my rhythm and tempo during the swing. The simplicity helped guide my grip and address the body/arm connection, which the instructor had ground into my head. His charismatic teaching method had empowered me, and I made the first hole in five strokes. My husband clapped and also glanced at me suspiciously. We played five more holes, so far so good; I'd discovered my passion.

On my next play, I sliced the ball.

"Fore, left!" I shouted. I thought I'd tweaked my swing,

but halfway to the green the ball curved, causing it to soar left over a hill, slide down an embankment, and sink into the awaiting pond.

"Oh, no," I cried. My husband shook his head and made his swing, landing the ball five yards from the hole. He continued putting to finish the hole in three strokes. Then we both hopped into the cart and drove up the hill. We treaded carefully down to the water. There, Jeff confirmed I'd suffer a one-point penalty retrieving my ball since I'd sunk it in a lateral water hazard. My heart lurched.

"How will I ever drive this ball back up the hill and reach hole number six?" I asked, trudging toward the pond. Amusement flickered in his eyes. Hesitant, I stuck my hand in the murky brownish pond and grabbed my ball.

Behind me, I heard an electric motor whining closer, making prickles stir on the back of my neck. I spun around and saw our golf cart speeding down the hill making a beeline for the pond. We both raced out of the way and watched the cart rush toward the edge, flip over, and splash wildly.

"Oops," I said, moisture collecting on my brow. "What do we do now?" Tears stung my eyes, but I pasted a smile on my face. I looked at Jeff and saw his mouth hanging wide open. A couple of golfers, clubs in hand, jogged over the hill.

"Are you two okay?" one shouted.

"Yes, but not my new cart," Jeff answered, weakly.

"You're supposed to avoid hitting the ball into the water trap and certainly not dunk your cart," a husky male voice said. Shards of laughter followed. At that moment, I wished I'd become invisible and swallowed a moan. Jeff gave me a sheepish grin and then joined in the laughter.

Someone phoned the clubhouse, and within fifteen minutes another golf cart and driver arrived; soon after, a tow truck followed. The cart guy questioned us and scribbled up an accident report. We both signed and he advised us to finish our game with the cart he'd driven.

As it turned out, the pond wasn't very deep and this wasn't the first time a cart went in for a swim. I watched the truck driver wade in wearing thigh-high boots and attach chains to our cart. As the motor sucked the cart from the pond, excess water drained from each doorway.

In the end, Jeff didn't blame me. The angle of the hill was very steep, and somehow the brake had slipped. At home, I apologized profusely and then confessed to Jeff about taking the golf lessons. He'd wondered how I'd played so well. The repair company notified us that the cart would take several days to dry, but it could be salvaged. In the meantime, Jeff rented carts for his golfing excursions.

The whole episode almost discouraged my newfound passion. A week later, Jeff prodded me to join him for a game. I swallowed hard, but finally agreed. Practice makes perfect, or so they say. I decided facing the course again was better than being a golfer's widow, but I vowed never to drive the cart again.

Suzanne Baginskie

"You always tell me it's only a game."

Come On In, the Water's Fine

For with God, nothing shall be impossible.

Luke 1:37

I was contemplating playing in my first charity golf tournament when I glanced out the kitchen window just in time to see a baby wren perch on the edge of our birdbath. Like a race car driver gunning her engines before takeoff, she was mimicking the motions she would need to bathe . . . over and over . . . before she even got wet. "Act as if" is a powerful principle. After much effort, the feisty little creature took the plunge. By this time her wings were so well practiced that she roared across the birdbath like a windup toy and promptly crashed into the far side. Two feathered friends watched in horror. Bristling her feathers, she regrouped and launched again, plowing a furrow across the small pond and thoroughly spraying her audience. Like the wren's swimming lesson, my golf game was not professional, but I was determined that I, too, would just keep doing what I'd been taught and dare to get wet. Hopefully I wouldn't drench the gallery! More importantly, I would have challenged my comfort zone, gotten some exercise, and, once again, walked by faith.

The day of the tournament dawned clear and WARM. I consoled myself that with a select-shot format, maybe I wouldn't be too much of a liability. A couple of times my shot was even chosen! Most of all, my husband and I enjoyed an afternoon together supporting a good cause and laughing with two previously unknown teammates who quickly became friends. At the last tee, however, I was hot, tired, and a little discouraged. My methods were not working. "God," I said, "I know this is only a game, and we are not in contention for a prize, but it sure would mean a lot if I could do just one thing that would make me feel I had helped my team."

None of us had ever played this course before. After my husband's second shot lofted up and over a hill, heading full speed toward the green, we all picked up our balls and crested the hill to play the ball on the . . . green? Regrettably, our "select shot" had rolled off the green and down a steep, fifteen-foot embankment into a sand trap! Three attempts before me had failed to clear the imposing incline. So the rookie reared back and swung with all her might. Miraculously the ball popped out of the sand and kept climbing just high enough to grab hold of the fringe of that elevated green. Much laughter ensued. Since I was the only one with a mulligan left, I scampered up the steep hill to make the first putt. Thirty feet of undulating green separated me from the hole. Oh well! I struck the ball and watched it roll . . . and roll . . . and roll . . . all the way down the hill . . . right into the hole! Again, riotous laughter and an unforgettable moment shared by all, compliments of a heavenly Father who rewards faith the size of a mustard seed, even the faith of a little bird.

Marcia Swearingen

6

JOY AND SORROW

Theme: Golf Causes Us to Experience a Full Range of Emotions

As you walk down the fairway of life you must smell the roses, for you only get to play one round.

Ben Hogan

Augusta Amen

The events of childhood do not pass but repeat themselves like seasons of the year.

Eleanor Farjeon

As a teenager, I left North Carolina to board full-time at the IMG David Leadbetter Golf Academy in Florida for my high school years. With eight girls to a dormitory room, we lived a structured life of school classes, golf instruction, workouts, and study hall. It was the same routine every day. So it was a relief when my dad arrived during my junior year to whisk me away for the weekend.

"Come on," he ordered, "we're flying to Georgia."

"Georgia?"

"Yeah," a wide grin swept his face, "wanna play a round at Augusta?"

Did I! What a thrill that would be.

Memories crowded my mind. I was perched on Dad's shoulders to watch the Masters at the Augusta National Golf Club . . . and see Jose Maria Olazabal win. Then, when I was bigger, standing in the crowds with my cardboard periscope and thinking it was the most amazing thing I'd ever seen. The course was perfect; the crowd magnificent; the energy indescribable. I pictured Nick Faldo walking off the eighteenth green with his caddy, Fanny. Because females were sparse on the course, I had bypassed Nick and walked right up to Fanny, asking for her autograph on my visor.

And now here we were again, driving down Magnolia Lane. My dad, his coach friend Dick Hill, and me. *Wow, I thought, only a few select people get the chance to make this drive. How lucky am I?*

We met up with my dad's friend, a club member who showed us around.

My eyes widened at the Masters trophy perched in the middle of the clubhouse, the life-sized portrait of founder Bobby Jones, and even the Crow's Nest where competing amateurs stayed. I poked my head into the Champions Locker Room—although it was probably against the rules.

We played the par three course first. It was, I knew, where they held the pre-Masters championships. Now here I was, playing it, too.

Then we teed up on the *real* course.

The exclusive Augusta National, I knew, had been named the finest course in the world by several of the best shot-makers. Annually hosting the most coveted tournament in professional golf, the club claimed some of the toughest holes to be found. Most famous was the Amen Corner, which included holes eleven, twelve, and thirteen.

I stood at the back tee of the first hole, recalling all the legendary golfers I'd seen tee off this same piece of grass on Masters Sunday. More than a bit nervous, I hit a strong drive straight down the middle with a slight fade. I hit my approach shot onto the green. *This isn't so hard,* I thought.

But my caddy eyed the twenty-five feet to the cup and warned, "Your first putt will have a quick pace to it."

Did it ever! I hit the putt at least twenty feet past the

hole . . . the first of *four* putts on that green. While my dad and the caddy chuckled under their breaths, I humbled my teenaged attitude and renewed my respect for both the course and the professional players who had conquered these links.

With not a cloud in the sky, it was a perfect February day. Like flawless carpet, the grass cushioned my stride as we played the round. At each hole we reminisced about legendary greats, chronicled their historic shots—and even attempted to replay them.

When we reached the Amen Corner, I was safe and sound on the eleventh green, which put me at ease. On the twelfth, I fired an eight iron right at the stick to about fifteen feet then drained it for birdie.

Still awed that I was actually playing Augusta, I closed my eyes and inhaled. I could almost smell the millions of egg salad and pimento cheese sandwiches consumed there each year by the grandstand galleries.

Near the fifteenth hole, Dad retold the story of Gene Sarazen's double eagle in 1935. "The shot heard around the world," he reminded me.

I tingled with a hazy infusion of time and the great golf moments that had occurred on this course. *Can it get it better than this?* I wondered.

And then we reached one of the most famous par threes in all of golf—the sixteenth. I knew the Masters had been won and lost on this very hole.

The sixteenth green could be forgiving or demanding. It all depended on where the pin placement happened to be—and I was 175 yards from the pin, which was back left on top of a mound. I frowned at the water bounding that entire side and following the sweep of green to the top. I wanted the shot to land somewhere on the upper tier; otherwise it might roll to the front of the green and create a tough lag putt.

I focused. I swung. And I hit my five iron pure.

The ball landed into the mound, bounced up . . . and rolled right into the hole, the famous par three hole, the grueling sixteenth.

I'd just made a hole in one! Unbelievable.

My dad, his friends, and the caddy went crazy with elation while I stood there, stunned.

The Augusta National, I thought, *and I had just aced the sixteenth hole.* It was almost more than I could absorb.

That night, we celebrated with dinner at the clubhouse, where I was treated like royalty. The pros from the shop claimed I was the only female to make a hole in one from the back tee on the sixteenth. They praised the seventy-six I'd shot. They took my picture. They mounted my ball and scorecard onto a crested Augusta plaque.

It was a plaque commemorating my own small slice of history at the notable Augusta National.

Perry Swenson

Hookers

I was on the driving range, hitting a bucket of balls at my old club, the club where I first learned to play golf. I heard a golf cart approach and turned to look over my shoulder. "I knew I recognized that swing," said the man sitting in the cart, a big grin on his face. It was Larry. I knew him almost at once.

It had been many years since I'd last seen him. Sure, he was weathered, and his blond hair had turned to gray, but he still had the same wide smile. Larry Bartosek had taught me to play golf. It was because of him, really, that I was here slugging my way through yet another bucket of balls.

Slowly he eased out of his seat and came over and gave me a hug. I was happy to see him after so many years, years in which I had married, had kids, gained some weight, lost some weight, switched careers a few times, and moved my blue sofa way too often. Finally, I was full circle, back to take some lessons from the current pro.

For many, it is their parents who get them hooked on golf, fathers who shove a golf club in their kids' hands when they can hardly stand up; mothers who drive them back and forth for their lessons. In my case, to my dad a wedge was a piece of pie. As for my mom, her idea of fun was to stencil the kitchen cabinets. Golf was simply not on our family radar.

I got the hook one hot July day when I was twelve and Larry, then the club pro, was running his kids' clinics. These were the days before video analysis, Great Big Berthas, and three-and-one-quarter-inch tees.

Slowly he moved down the line, showing us how to grip the club and hit balls that frequently did not fly as far as the divots. When he got to me he said, "Ever play golf before?"

"Nope," I said, probably with a snotty what-do-I-care attitude.

"You should. You have a natural swing."

That did it. That was the hook. My ego swelled. I'm not sure which came first, the huge crush I had on him or my parents agreeing to let me take golf lessons. My interest in the game grew as Larry patiently led me through the fundamentals, encouraging me when I groaned at a poorly hit ball . . . "That's O.K. Try again." Then, "Good shot." I needed a lot of back scratching.

I started playing in some junior tournaments and actually won a couple. I remember my first golf gear: a set of Patty Berg clubs and a green nylon bag with tan leather trim. For the next couple of years, Larry was there to boost my morale, take a look at my swing when it went totally south, and remind me how to get out of bunkers. He even tried to get me to practice.

I hated practicing. Besides, endless phone conversations with girlfriends and school stuff didn't leave much time for practice. And because I could hit the ball farther than most of the other girls at the club, many older than I was, I had acquired a certain obnoxious, cocky smugness. Of course, the fact that I didn't ever know where it was going, or why, occasionally took a bite out of my confidence. Consistency? Not there. My drives on the second hole landed way too often in the horse pasture, an out-of-bounds running along the right side of the fairway. I was afraid of horses, so I lost a lot of balls.

Still, golf was fun those years, playing with friends, competing in the club tournaments. I loved that rush when match play got down to two holes and I was tied with my opponent, my adrenaline running.

Then life became cheerleading practice, waterskiing, parties. The green nylon golf bag and Patty Berg clubs propped up against the wall in the basement acquired a patina of dust.

In college, just for kicks, I tried out for the college golf team and made it. Not that it was any big deal. I think that everyone who went out for golf at Denison made the team. But I started playing again, practicing, and trying to recall the things Larry had told me. Gradually it dawned on me that, indeed, Larry had given me something very precious: a confidence that it was possible for me to play golf, and even play it well if I was willing to take the time.

So there it was, always dangling out there like the brass ring on the carousel. All I had to do was take the game seriously and I could do it. Some years I played a lot, joined the women's league, and saw my handicap creep down. Even the years when I didn't play much, I knew that whenever I did get out there, I could enjoy hitting the ball without totally embarrassing myself.

So here I was, oh-so-many years later, determined once again to improve my game. And here once again was Larry, still upbeat, still smiling and encouraging. For sure, whatever he had set in motion when I was a kid continues to enhance my life.

Chances are, if you love golf, you too will recall with fondness, even joy, the person who first got you hooked on the game.

Sure, Larry has changed, but haven't we all? He's retired but scoring close to his age. And here I am, still trying to figure out how to hit the ball consistently so I wouldn't want to dig a hole for myself on the first tee.

Some things just don't change.

Katharine Dyson

Sand Trap Isn't the Biggest Hazard McGann Faces

It is hard to believe that Michelle McGann has ever had the shakes while standing over a putt. After all, you don't win seven Ladies Professional Golf Association (LPGA) Tour tournaments—including three in one year—if you have the nerves of a jackrabbit.

Golfers call a shaky putting stroke the "yips." But that isn't what has made Michelle's knees turn to Jell-O and her mouth go dry. Mere pressure doesn't make her head spin and ache. After all, her nickname rightly should be "Ms. Clutch."

To give you an idea, Michelle has been in four LPGA playoffs—the ultimate pressure cooker—and won all four times. It is the best mark in LPGA history.

No, Michelle's problem on the golf course has never been mental. She has never had a fear of failure, just a fear of falling.

Michelle, you see, is a diabetic.

In addition to worrying about exact yardage to the green, she has to concern herself with precise blood sugar levels. Mind you, a miscalculation on a four-iron approach shot might result in the ball landing in the bunker, but an error in her insulin level might result in Michelle landing in the hospital.

That is no exaggeration. In 1999, Michelle's insulin pump became dislodged during a tournament round, and she went nearly eight hours without an injection. As a result, her blood sugar level shot up above 1,000. Normal is between 70 and 120.

"It hit me suddenly," Michelle recalls.

Luckily her mom was with her at the time. Even luckier, Bernadette McGann is a nurse. She knew what to do—get her daughter to the emergency room as quickly as possible.

"We didn't even wait for an ambulance," Michelle shares. "I almost went into a diabetic coma. The doctor said I could have died."

To be sure, Michelle's biggest challenge isn't par, or sand and trees, or water guarding the front of the green. It's her endocrine system. It's a hazard you can't avoid by aiming left or laying up short.

In addition to carrying fourteen clubs in her golf bag, she has to have extra insulin—also power bars and peanut butter sandwiches.

Michelle found out she was diabetic at age thirteen. It didn't slow her down or make her golf scores go up. She became a three-time Florida State Junior Champion, the 1987 USGA Junior Girls Champion, and the AJGA Rolex Junior Player of the Year before turning pro at age eighteen in 1989.

Michelle didn't just master all of the golf shots, but also how to administer shots of insulin. Rolling putts with touch is difficult enough without your fingertips being all scarred up from constantly being pricked to take blood sugar readings.

A few years ago, the five-foot, eleven-inch Michelle made a big change. Not to an oversized driver or new putter. She switched from two insulin shots a day to wearing a computerized pump the size of a beeper that administers hourly dosages.

The initial results weren't spectacular. In fact, 1999 was her worst season on the Tour in ten years as she finished seventy-second on the money list. It was a big drop after six straight years in the top twenty, including ranking number seven and number eight in 1995 and 1996.

Well. Michelle McGann added a new club in her bag, so to speak, in 2001. To help fine-tune her insulin pump, she wore a second minicomputer that recorded her blood sugar level every five minutes. The stored data was then used to design a program of insulin injections that best suited her.

It was like a caddie handing her the perfect club for the distance at hand. Michelle went out and had six top-ten finishes, including a third-place showing that featured her first hole in one. She also led the Tour in eagles and climbed to number thirty-one on the season money list.

"The insulin pump is awesome," says Michelle, who is known for her bright lipstick and brighter smile. "It made golf fun again. Before, I was focusing so much on having perfect blood sugars that I think I was losing my focus on golf."

The cup started looking big again. In 2001, Michelle shot a final-round sixty-four to earn a runner-up trophy, and in 2002 had the second hole in one of her career. In 2005 she surpassed $3.2 million in lifetime earnings.

"It's amazing what making a few putts will do," she said, explaining her renewed success. Of course, it's easier to make putts now that her head doesn't turn dizzy from a crashing blood sugar level.

With her high-tech help, she no longer is in effect giving up two strokes a side to the competition.

The LPGA media guide shows that Michelle McGann has yet to win one of the four "major" tournaments. That's really not quite accurate: every time she tees up, it's a major victory.

Woody Woodburn

Shooting Par on the Eighteenth

When my husband had a heart attack and was put on disability, he started playing golf. His best friend, Don, taught him how. His bad ticker meant that he had to ride in a cart, but swinging the clubs and the little bit of walking from the cart to the tee or the green was good for him.

After a time, I got a job that left me free much of the afternoon each day of the week. Bill and I went to Swannanoa Country Club where he had his membership, and he began teaching me to play. As it turned out, I could hit the ball with the men distancewise, but I had one heck of a slice. Bill would tell me to try this, that, and the other, but nothing seemed to help. Finally I took lessons, and that straightened out my slice—sometimes.

Much of the time we argued a great deal about my slice and how I should fix it, or why I couldn't track my own ball after I hit it. (Turns out I have a problem with my eyes not refocusing quickly enough to see the darn thing.)

Now, in those days, Swannanoa was a two-man operation, and the course was never crowded because it was not well-maintained and there were several prime courses in the area. It was our treasure and our pleasure. On weekends in the spring, we often played into the fog that would settle on the mountaintop. It wasn't too much of a problem since we knew where the pin was and how far we had to hit it.

The bane of my existence on that course was the eighteenth hole. It was a very long par five with a dogleg right and slanted to the right, where there was a narrow rough and then the road beyond that. My tee shot often landed in the rough, or just as often in the road. We probably argued about how I should play that hole more than any other. Most times, I took my nine strokes and we headed for the clubhouse.

Early in the morning one Friday in June, Bill's heart finally gave out. I was at his side as he passed peacefully.

Our membership was good through that summer, and after a while I began to go up alone and play nine holes. I felt close to him there. The first time I played the back nine and came to the eighteenth, I couldn't help shuddering. That hole had always defeated me, and although I thought this time would be no different, I was determined to give it my best shot.

I lined up my tee shot slightly left as Bill had made me practice and whacked that ball a country mile. I could see its general direction, which looked pretty good. I walked along the fairway, around that curve, and to my great surprise, there was my little white ball almost perfectly in the middle. My second shot brought me nearly to the apron, and it took me one more shot to reach the green. I two-putted and parred that darn hole.

I went into the clubhouse for a Coke and the pro asked me how I did.

"I parred eighteen," I said. "It was the very first time."

"Good for you. Bill would have been proud."

Yes, he would, I thought. But he still would have grinned and said, "I told you so."

Cary Osborne

More Than Coincidence

First and foremost, you must believe in yourself. You must always pursue quality and have integrity, perseverance, and, of course, the desire to succeed.

Greg Norman

There's one more left. One more ball that Ollie gave me, I thought. Ollie loved playing golf, and in the last couple of years his cancer went into remission long enough for him to get back out on the course. He had his share of birdies and even scored an eagle once, but that elusive hole in one remained just that—elusive.

I took up golfing years ago as a way to enjoy the pastime with him. We traveled all the way to Scotland one year and played the courses of old. And for many years we had been coming to one of the Hawaiian Islands to play the prestigious courses Ollie loved. But he was gone now, and I was traveling alone. It was hard to join the others on the first trip after he died.

That afternoon started out with a few sprinkles in the

air. "How are you doing?" my friend Sue asked me as I joined up to ride with her in the cart.

"I'm fine," I said, but I had to admit to myself that I was more than a little shaken. I thought of the light rain as love showers from Ollie. I swallowed hard and fought back the tears.

We made it through the first nine holes. I had brought a sleeve of balls with me that morning, the last sleeve of Ollie's from when he used to play. But I had already lost two of them.

Now, as I rolled the last ball into my hand, I held it tight. I grabbed a tee and my club. I approached the tee box and lined up my shot. It was a short hole, just eighty-six yards. I brought the club head back and made a normal swing, but then something happened that had never happened before. The ball sailed into the air, straight at the flagstick. It landed, rolled, and dropped right into the hole.

A hole in one! A hole in one! Ollie, you finally got your hole in one! As my shouts and laughter rang throughout the golf course, I felt the patter of a softly falling rain. I turned my face to the sky and let the sprinkles mesh with my tears. Ollie was with me, in heaven and on earth. Of that I was certain.

Rosie Farley
As told to B. J. Taylor

Surviving the Challenge

*Don't hurry. Don't worry. You're only here for
a short visit. So don't forget to stop and smell the
roses.*

Walter Hagen

My love for golf started when I was ten years old. My
parents encouraged me to learn how to play, so I could
spend family time with them. I became obsessed and challenged by this amazing game. Since golf is an individual
sport, I could play and practice anytime I desired. I
devoted hours every day to practicing the skills that were
taught to me, and I dreamed of playing golf on the tour
before I found my niche teaching golf and helping others.
Golf is much more than a game to me, and I have learned
many skills from this "work in progress." Discipline, dedication, determination, and patience are a few. I have
learned all of these life skills from playing and teaching
golf, and they have helped me deal with various personal
issues and health challenges.

In the winter of my tenth year teaching golf, I was
diagnosed with breast cancer. A "divot" was carved out of

my breast and death surrounded me, as I lost both my bio-logical father and stepfather earlier that year. My close friend Heather Farr, a Ladies Professional Golf Association (LPGA) tour player, died of breast cancer a week before I was diagnosed. My children were nine and five years old. I wondered how I would tell them about my diagnosis and the possibility of life without their mom. This horrible disease forced me to change my perception of life. I reached deep within my soul and chose to "live in the moment" every day and make the best of each situation regardless of how hard it was. Enjoying the "dance" of life kept me positive during my fight. I kept focused on the beauty that surrounded me: nature, love, and support from my family and friends. I became passionate to play and teach golf again.

After the lumpectomy and radiation, I slowly became active again. Fortunately, I am right-handed, and it was my left side that was affected by the surgery. After three months of therapy I was ready to start playing golf again. Since I couldn't feel the underside of my left arm, my golf swing became foreign to me. Fortunately, however, I had practiced my swing so much in my younger years that my muscle memory kicked in. It was hard to generate power on my weaker left side, which resulted in a loss of distance in my golf shots, but I was so driven by my excitement to play golf again that I kept searching for ways to build strength in my body.

I started to teach golf again that spring and it felt so good to be back in my "beautiful office." I appreciated the chance to help people improve their golf skills, and it was even more rewarding to watch them succeed. I became more sensitive to physical limitations and learned to cus-tomize a swing for each individual. Being a survivor of breast cancer was frightening, yet powerful. It is very similar to hitting a golf shot. If you are fearful about a shot, you are more likely to tense up and cause a bad result. If you can trust and be confident in your plan to execute a particular swing, you will have a better chance to react properly and create a successful shot. Knowing what to perform in a golf shot gives you courage and confidence to trust and believe it will happen. This was the lesson I learned from playing and teaching golf, and it has helped me deal with my fear of breast cancer.

Nine months later, I was involved in an accident that resulted in a head injury. I suffered a stroke and had to have brain surgery. I thought I had learned a lot from dealing with breast cancer; however, I now faced two new and different challenges—short-term memory loss and baldness. Fear consumed me as the doctor unveiled my head. I discovered that I was bald, had a horseshoe-shaped scar, and four titanium screws in my head. I wondered what people would think of my new appearance. My pride as a female was stripped twofold. I was now bald and had lost half of one breast. Slowly I realized I may never play or teach golf again. Depression and fear enveloped me; two life challenges nine months apart were almost too much to deal with. I truly believe that the skills I learned from golf helped me overcome both of these challenges.

Through golf I had learned dedication and perseverance. I was always committed to being the best I could be, and never giving up. Using these skills I learned how to practice each facet of golf and keep "grinding" even if there was no immediate positive result. The same now applied to my life! I wanted to play and teach golf so badly that I had to become totally focused on my goal. I designed a step-by-step plan of action to achieve my goals. Cognitive therapy helped push my brain to new frontiers, and I learned how to listen to my body. I was completely committed and kept "grinding" through physical pain, doubt, and constant frustration. Life is a very bumpy road. So far it has taught me that nothing is forever. You must live your life one day at a time and be the best person you can be physically, mentally, and emotionally. Golf is an amazing game! It can help you discover yourself, and it can provide you with skills to deal with whatever life throws your way. I feel so blessed to have found this game and learned so many lessons from it.

I am a thirteen-year breast cancer survivor and am still enjoying this "beautiful walk in the park" we call golf! I have survived the challenge!

Ann Wolta

If There Is Golf in Heaven, I Know My Sister Sue Is Playing

The fairway of life leads us down many paths—knowing which one to take is the greatest mystery. As I sit at Sue's funeral, trying to find the right words to express my fondest memories of her, I find myself remembering her passion for golf. She truly loved playing the game. And I chuckle to myself wondering who would have thought that someday I too would have found that same passion?

This story is about two sisters and how the game of golf and the tragedy of life rekindled their love and friendship. My name is Pam and I'm the oldest of eight children; my sister Sue was the baby girl. We grew up in a loving and close family. To us, our family was perfect. Life seemed great, but as some things seem too good to be true, it certainly was. Our family was living with a terrible curse, a disease called amyotrophic lateral sclerosis (ALS), better known as Lou Gehrig's disease. It is an incurable disease that robs your muscles of movement, to the point that you become a prisoner in your own body. Not knowing this, or what lay ahead for our family—let alone Sue's destiny—our lives went on.

She was only ten when she started to play golf. In my father's eyes, it was only a boy's sport, but that didn't stop Sue. She had the desire and the determination to play, especially against the boys. I, on the other hand, being twenty-three at the time, thought golf was just a foolish way to chase a little white ball down the fairway. I was too busy being married and raising a family.

When Sue was about fourteen, my father's job transferred the family to Germany. Only the four youngest children and my mom went. The rest of the family was all married or going to college. It was a very trying time in Sue's life. She was attending junior high and didn't want to leave the friends she had made, let alone the rest of us. Sue needed to find something to keep her mind off of home, so she started playing golf again. It became her release. I remember when she took first place in a junior championship division, and won the title Best of Europe. We were all so proud of her.

About ten years later, just when life seemed to become normal again, my father became very ill. He was stricken with ALS. Not only did this devastate the family, but at the same time we found out it was hereditary. This was more than Sue could bear. She became very distraught, sadly losing the desire to play golf or to be around the family. I guess, in her eyes, she thought if she wasn't close to anyone anymore it wouldn't hurt as much when someone else died. They say once your parents die, the family has a tendency to split up. Being the oldest, I always felt the need to keep the family together.

Looking back now, and maybe this was fate and not knowing where my path was leading me, my husband and I bought a house on a golf course, and to my family's surprise, I started playing golf.

The year was 1999, and I remember that day very well.

My club was putting on a ladies' invitational, and I needed to find a partner to participate. I quickly remembered Sue. I thought, *Man, what a great way to get her involved with the family again and have a great golfing partner at the same time.* I was so proud having my little sister playing golf with me. No one knew how good she was. She was my secret weapon, my little ringer, and because of her, we won second place. That year was our first invitational and the beginning of our special bond together.

As the years went on, we played five more invitationals together, managing to take second or third place each year. The year 2005, our sixth year playing together, will be embedded in my memory forever. Unbeknownst to us, this year was the beginning of Sue's ALS. She started to have trouble with her strength. Her drives weren't going as far. Never in our worst fears did we think the disease was causing this. I remember how she kept on getting down on herself, thinking she wasn't trying her best. I tried to reassure her that she didn't have to worry; she was my partner, and it was about time for me to carry her. My love for my sister gave me strength to pull the team together; it was the best round I ever played. I guess that is what partners are for. That year we missed winning the championship by one point. But, you know, it really didn't matter to us, for in our hearts, we became first place in SISTER'S.

In January 2006, at the young age of forty-six, Sue sadly passed away. I know life goes on, and it seems very hard some days to get by, so I've taken a lesson from my baby sister and I let the game of golf be my release. I will never forget how much fun Sue and I had playing golf together, especially our invitational. Oh, by the way, Sue, if you are playing golf in heaven, could you please let God win now and then?

Pamela M. Woods

7

TOMORROW'S TEE TIME

Theme: Golf Is a Game of Constant Renewal, Learning, and Unending Optimism

Keep your sense of humor. There's too much stress in the rest of your life to let bad shots ruin a game you're supposed to enjoy.

Amy Alcott

Little White Golf Ball

Little white golf ball
please tell me of the trick
to hitting you down the middle with this skinny little
     stick.

I try to keep my left arm straight—
my head is always down—
but still I see my best attempt go dribbling on the
     ground.

Why do I pull you to the left,
or slice you to the right?
What will it take to hit you straight until you're out of
     sight?

The money spent on lessons—
all the practice balls I hit—
only add to my frustration
when it doesn't help a bit.

For even when I do things right
it only lasts awhile.
It never seems like very long
before I lose my smile.

So little white golf ball
please tell me of the trick
to hitting you down the middle with this skinny little
    stick.

Tom Krause

The Luck of the Irish

My worst day of golf still beats my best day at the office.

John Hallisey

Most people associate golf with St. Andrews in Scotland, the "home of golf." However, I now associate golf with St. Patrick's Day, a fun holiday I've always observed even though I'm not Irish.

As a high school vice principal, I often showed up at school with cookies covered with green sprinkles to celebrate St. Patrick's Day. I'd string my office with green lights left over from Christmas. I'd wear green clothing onto which I'd faithfully pin my flashing, battery-operated shamrock. No, I'm not Irish, but I'm also not stupid. No way would I ever put myself in a position to be pinched by playful students waiting to take advantage of my forgetfulness to wear green. Mainly, though, I looked forward to this grand day because it was a break from the pressures of life as a vice principal.

March 17, 1998, proved to be an exception. I called in to take that day off. It's called a "personal necessity" day, but it was really me playing hooky from school. The stress from work had been intense that year, dealing with fights, expulsions, and disgruntled parents. I desperately needed some downtime—even if it meant I'd miss the festivities of St. Patrick's Day. So I took the day off and headed to the golf course with my husband, Bud, who had retired two years before.

Bud has played golf all of his life. When we met, he taught me how to play. Because of my heavy work schedule, I could never find the time to give it much attention, so I never seemed to get better at it. But I liked going to the golf course. I enjoyed being outdoors, surrounded by trees and wildlife. The entire experience relaxed me. And once in a while when I'd hit a great shot, it would inspire me to want to come back for more.

So there we were on the fourth hole of the Sun City Timbers Creek golf course in Roseville, California, when I punched the ball with my Light & Easy seven wood onto the green ninety-five yards away. The ball took two bounces and started tracking toward the cup.

"Go in the hole! Go in the hole!" Bud shouted, staring at the ball, which disappeared from sight. Two residents, who had been watching from their backyard, jumped up and yelled, "We'll be your witness!" Stumped, I quickly asked Bud, "What do I need a witness for?"

"You just made a hole in one! Anyone can claim they've made a hole in one, so witnesses are now required to prove it."

Talk about mixed reactions. First, I was stunned as I retrieved the ball from the hole. What a surreal moment that was. I had accomplished something in a few years that Bud in his fifty years of playing golf had not. A hole in one! Wow! It was unbelievable. I sensed Bud was a bit jealous. I was beginning to feel special, but not for long. I soon became chagrined because I knew it had nothing to do with skill. It was dumb luck, really. It was a fluke. A random act of kindness bestowed on me by the golf gods.

Second, I was worried. "Don't tell anybody about this," I said to Bud. "I don't want to have to buy everybody drinks at the bar." I'd always thought golf was expensive enough without having to cave in to its notorious traditions. Besides, we hadn't bothered to buy hole in one insurance, anyway.

Finally, I was afraid. Afraid people would think I was good at golf. What a laugh! Afraid I'd be expected to do it again. Another laugh! Afraid my colleagues at work would find out that I'd played hooky that day. What kind of dedicated educator was I to leave my faculty members in the lurch when my presence was needed on campus on such a potentially rowdy occasion?

The next day at school I was in the mail room when one of the football coaches walked in to get his mail. "Was that you I read about in the paper this morning?" he asked. "Did you get the hole in one?"

My cheeks burned from embarrassment. I'd been found out. "Yeah, that was me," I said, wondering how it had appeared in the newspaper. Turns out the golf pro had given my husband a fourth-hole flag in the pro shop, which Bud later had embroidered with the date as a souvenir for me. The golf pro had called the hole in one in to the local paper.

"Well, give me five!" the coach roared, extending his hand up in the air for a high five. As other staff poured through the mail room and into the teacher's lounge, I could hear him telling them about my good news. The reaction was all the same: cheers, bravos, congratulations.

I was floored. No one berated me for taking the day off. No one even missed me. Not only had I escaped getting into trouble, I was the new hero on campus, admired and respected. Much envied. Somehow I had reached the pinnacle of the average golfer's highest achievement.

Although the faculty attributed my success to out-standing athletic ability, I knew better. No, it was something altogether different. All my years of celebrating St. Patrick's Day had finally paid off. The luck of the Irish—at long last—had rubbed off on me.

Jennifer Martin

"You wouldn't punish a person
for making a hole in one would you?"

Mastering the Game

Open up a local Augusta, Georgia, paper anytime of the year and you are bound to see ads requesting tickets for a major unnamed sporting event. Then, as the first week in April approaches, golfers desperate to obtain a coveted badge begin arriving in town in hordes. These devoted fanatics brave the elements in a last-ditch effort to obtain a ticket to that unnamed event. They sit in collapsible chairs on the sides of the most well-traveled roads and hold up signs: "Will Work for Tickets," "Will Pay Any Price for Tickets," "Praying for Tickets"—and I cannot help but feel a stab of guilt, for I spent most of my life saying, "No, thank you" to that which they so desperately seek.

I spent my early childhood living in a house less than a mile from the Augusta National. Every year, our dear neighbors offered my parents the use of their badges, and every year, my parents politely declined. Neither of them were golfers, nor did they possess any real interest in the sport. In fact, that week was simply a nuisance to us. For days, we were practically prisoners in our own home. Any outing had to be carefully timed in order to avoid the long traffic delays, and Daddy was forced to leave for work long before usual in order to circumvent the traffic jams that inevitably occurred right in front of our house.

Even after we moved to the suburbs, a mere twenty-minute drive from the main entrance to the course, we turned down invitations to attend the golfing event. By then, I was a teenager, and my regular babysitting customers were always far more generous that week. During off-hours, I headed in the opposite direction, toward the lake to be with my friends. I preferred bikinis to the conservative attire of the golf patrons, and beach balls and volley balls won out over golf balls, hands down!

I was an adult before I finally succumbed to the pressure and accepted an invitation to attend the tournament. My husband and I fought the traffic, paid an exorbitant parking fee, and made the long trek to the entry gate. The moment we entered that course, however, it was as if we had been transformed to another place and time. I had no idea that in the midst of our sprawling little metropolis, a place of such beauty existed. Undulating, gentle hills of green punctuated by vibrant bursts of color greeted us. Tall pines and dogwoods bursting with blossoms seemed to touch the sky. Curious turtles popped their heads out of the ponds, perhaps the only casual observers for whom badges were not required. And though I was not an avid follower of the game, the simple grandeur of the clubhouse and a glance at the famous Magnolia Lane was truly a spectacle to behold. It was simply breathtaking.

We spent the day wandering the course, marveling, not necessarily at the famed golfers, but at the natural beauty that surrounded us. We ate our creamy pimento cheese sandwiches underneath the shade of a tall pine and whiled away the hours watching people walk by, wondering just who might be sitting beside us or walking among us. When we finally hiked back to the car and reentered the real world outside the gates, I had a deeper understanding of just what it is that attracts so many people to a town like Augusta, Georgia, in April of each year.

I have attended the Masters on several occasions since then. Most years, however, the entire family, all of whom still live within minutes of the course, still opts to leave town for the duration of the tournament. We cannot help but prefer the seclusion of the coast to the traffic and mayhem that comes with the tournament. However, if we do stay in town, I am less inclined to turn down an invitation to attend the famous golfing event. In fact, I think this will be a good year for a visit. I am far too old for a bikini, and I am ready to enjoy a good pimento cheese sandwich beneath a tall Georgia pine! It is a good year for golf!

Terri K. Duncan

A Humbling Lesson

When I met my husband, I was a tennis player. Golf made my short list of dull sports, lagging just behind drag racing and professional bowling. Despite my disdain, my husband-to-be proposed taking me out as a guest on his golf course to "play a few holes." Dogged by nature, I quickly became obsessed by the apparent ease, but practical impossibility, of hitting the golf ball in the air. I hacked my way along the first five fairways until my host implemented a ten-stroke-per-hole limit.

Two years later, I was a changed woman. I began to write about golf. I dreamed about golf. I taped obscure golf tournaments on TV (if I was out playing golf and unable to watch). At cocktail parties, while normal women chatted about their kids or their jobs, I could be found in a cluster of men rehashing their golfing exploits in tedious detail. I subjected my husband to eye-glazing replays of recent rounds. Our family room decor was early modern golf swing: a full-length mirror (to observe my swing), an automatic putting strip, a chipping net over the couch, an array of practice clubs and balls underfoot. My teenage stepchildren made scathing remarks about the importance that golf had assumed in my life, and by forced proximity, theirs.

Over time, by dint of hundreds of dollars worth of lessons and hours of practice, I managed to wrestle my handicap to the high teens. This allowed me to enter the Connecticut Women's Golf Association Championship qualifying event—I was riding high. I truly had no idea just how far over my head I would be.

The venue for the tournament that season, the Yale University golf course, begins with a 150-yard carry over water and a U.S. Open–style rough to a steep, uphill fairway. I watched a progression of the best amateur women golfers in the state get intimidated, and then humbled, by this tee. From my perspective in the final threesome, that first shot loomed larger and larger.

Though barely breathing when my turn came, I hit a passable drive, advanced the ball with a series of unattractive grounders, and chipped in for double bogey. Cruising through the eighth (famous for sand traps so deep there's a staircase to help you climb out) and the ninth holes (140 yards of pure carry over water), I began to imagine I might actually qualify. Which is when I should have remembered Sam Cheever's warning words: "Left to my own devices, my self-importance grows like pond scum."

On the twelfth tee, I yanked my drive into the woods: irretrievable. A second attempt squirted into waist-high grass. Flustered, I chopped at the barely visible ball, moving it five feet.

"Take an unplayable lie," whispered my caddie. I dropped back twenty feet and banged the ball into another patch of impassable rough. The other players and caddies averted their eyes as I carded a twelve and reeled to the next tee.

I needed emergency aid. As both a psychologist and golf fanatic, I had made a study of the mental side of golf.

This was the time to call on every tip I could remember. I attended to my tempo. I played one shot at a time. I leaned on my preshot routine. I scrambled to entertain only positive thoughts. I saw the target. I was the target. And I scored no better than triple bogey for the remainder of the round.

Even worse than facing the immediate reality of my poor performance, I was aware that my whopping score and embarrassing status in last place would appear the next morning in the local newspaper.

I was right. And my name, which is ordinarily butchered into hundreds of unrecognizable permutations—Alberto Isbeil, Rupert Sleiba, and so on—was spelled with inhuman precision: "ROBERTA ISLEIB-120."

With passing time, those memories have faded into a painful blur. (In other words, the entire humiliating back nine no longer flashes through my mind when I approach the first tee—any first tee.) And I've tried to make something useful out of the experience by extracting these palliative observations:

1. Golf, like life, is cruel and mercurial. Because your fortunes can change direction at any moment, both demand patience, humor, and humility.
2. Golf, like life, requires resilience. If you play a shot, a hole, or a round badly, learn from it and put it behind you. Be your own best friend on the course. Or as my golf psychologist friend Joseph Parent would say, fire your inner evil caddie.
3. Golf, like life, is addictive—a few great moments can erase a long, nightmarish stretch. That's why you'll find golfers who, ready to tag sale their clubs at the end of the round, are arranging games for the next morning by the time they arrive at the nineteenth hole.

Sports psychologists have named this phenomenon intermittent reinforcement. Nongolfers have a name for it too: foolishness. Marriage counselors would describe it as the triumph of hope over experience. It's all that, and more. It's golf.

I hate it. I love it. When's my tee time?

Roberta Isleib

"Gentlemen Only, Ladies Forbidden"

When I die bury me on the golf course so my husband will visit.

Author Unknown

I am a golf widow.

My husband is so obsessed by golf that he lives and breathes it. Golfing is in his blood. I blame it on his Scottish ancestry. It is said that the game originated in Scotland and was first called "Gentlemen Only, Ladies Forbidden," which is supposedly how the word "GOLF" entered into the English language.

What is golf, exactly? Some define it as an endless series of tragedies obscured by the occasional miracle. All I know is you hit down to make the ball go up, you swing left and the ball goes right, and the lowest score wins. On top of that, the winner buys the drinks.

I do not share my husband's passion. When he dragged me kicking and screaming to a driving range, my air shots gouged big chunks of grass into the wild blue yonder. I bailed out, which was probably a good thing for the course.

Golfing terminology is a mystery to me. When I hear of birdies and eagles, all that comes to mind is an aviary. Tee time, a sand wedge, and a slice have nothing to do with an afternoon snack. Discussions about handicaps, bogeys, and doglegs make my eyes start to glaze over. I am familiar with ball markers, although ball washers are an enigma. I won't even go there. An ace is a hole in one, but how can yelling "Fore!" alert others to an oncoming ball? Why not just yell, "Watch out, crooked shot coming!" Isn't a square stance when you swing your partner do-si-do? And the biggest conundrum: why is the club called a three wood when it is made of metal?

Golf courses in Winnipeg are only open about half the year, but there are other ways to indulge one's appetite for golf. True hackers practice their swing even as the snow falls. They have artificial putting greens in their basements. They play virtual golf, visit the golf dome, or try to beat Jack Nicklaus on the computer. They watch the Golf Channel religiously and worship Tiger Woods's every move. They buy golf magazines and gadgets, and when family members wonder what to buy for a gift, the standard reply is, "Get him a dozen golf balls; he will be thrilled." And he always is.

When the golf courses close for the winter, sometimes the golf addict in this family indulges his passion by going on a golf vacation to warmer climes. Then I end up listening to feverish, detailed descriptions of the thirty-six holes he played every day.

Excited husband: "I hit a long power fade that bounced twice and ended up stiff to the hole!"

Wife, yawning, feigning interest: "That's nice, dear."

"I was swinging over the top almost every day but my putter was saving me!"

"Yes, dear." Zzzz.

While in Florida, my husband almost hit an alligator

with a golf ball. Mr. Gator was dozing peacefully on the fairway, surrounded by several abandoned golf balls. Other duffers had wisely beat a hasty retreat, not even bothering to use their golf ball retrievers.

To appease the trauma, hubby treated himself to a new sand wedge. The airline prohibited him from carrying it on the plane, as it could be construed as a weapon, so he had to check it in as luggage. Wrapped carefully, the wedge traveled from Orlando to Toronto to Winnipeg, and arrived as broken as my husband's heart when he saw the damage. Fortunately the airline paid to have it repaired, at a greater cost than the purchase price of the club.

This man owns more golf shirts than underwear, and he sometimes wears strange combinations of colors because that is the golfer's way. He once had a pair of plum-colored golf pants with a golf shirt to match. After wearing this outfit several times, he discarded the pants because the fabric didn't breathe. I think his fellow golfers teasingly calling him "Barney" had something to do with it. Another thing I don't understand is why golf clothes are so expensive.

"Look honey, I got two new golf shirts and they were only seventy-five dollars each! What a bargain!"

What he spent on two shirts is what I spend on groceries for two weeks.

One year I bought him a new driver for Father's Day. He pronounced it too "whippy" and rarely used it. The following year, I tried to make up for my faux pas by buying him the book *Chicken Soup for the Golfer's Soul*. This was a big mistake. His attitude was that real men don't read Chicken Soup books any more than they eat quiche. This year he will get golf balls.

My husband's dream is to live on the links, with me as his caddie, but I'd rather languish on the nineteenth hole, reading my copy of *Chicken Soup for the Golf Widow's Soul*. A hand-painted sign in our house proclaims, "We interrupt this marriage for golf." No truer words were ever written.

And that's par for the course.

Maria Harden

Reprinted by permission of Joe Kohl. ©1996 Joe Kohl.

More Than a Game

It sounded like a bad mystery. Three sisters out on a golf course playing a competitive round of golf. Two are standing next to each other, while the third is behind the wheel of their cart. The day is progressing normally enough when suddenly the cart lurches out of control, and the one sister runs down one of the others. Someone who'd been listening to the scanner had heard an ambulance had been called. There were serious injuries. One of the sisters was in a lot of pain. The other had to be feeling pretty miserable too—unless she'd secretly nurtured some long-held and secret—or perhaps not-so-secret—grudge against her sister.

I am a pastor—I had only recently arrived at my latest posting. The church was located in the small town of Everett, set in the Pennsylvania portion of the Appalachians, once known by the more picturesque name of Bloody Run before the city fathers decided to name the town after the long-winded orator whose three-hour speech, delivered before the spare and unforgettable Gettysburg Address, is never remembered today.

I'm from the big city of Los Angeles, and I'd become

aware that small towns have unique problems of their own. Everyone knows everyone else, and resentments can fester over generations. Sometimes "accidents" happen, and a lot of the time nobody is really surprised!

I was still getting to know people. My first impression of Anna and Bev, the two sisters, had been mostly positive. Both were retired. They lived together, a very odd couple indeed. Bev was tall and angular, while Anna was extremely short, thanks to a medical condition that had caused an extreme curvature of the spine. Both seemed extremely intelligent, but I hadn't spoken to either long enough to know much of anything about them or their relationship.

Except I knew that they loved golf. I'd learned that way back when I first interviewed at the church. Because of her medical condition Anna had to drive a cart along the course, but I could tell that nothing stood in the way of her doing whatever she pleased, regardless of physical limitations.

Golf was a passion that drew them to the links.

And now this—I wanted the chance to get to know people before a major medical emergency threw me into the fray. I hadn't even preached yet.

The details were very sketchy. Anna had been driving her cart when Bev had been run down. She hadn't stopped the cart after striking her sister. Bev's shoulder was badly separated. Surgery was indicated. Therapy would follow. There might be severe internal injuries.

I sighed. At the very least I'd need to be doing some counseling, I assumed. There would be resentment, I was sure, because of the injury. This might reveal other, deeper wounds that would have to be healed. And then there would be the problem of guilt. Even if it were an accident, surely Anna would feel just awful about what happened. My experience is that guilt is much more damaging than actual pain or suffering. Even when a person has been for-given by an aggrieved party, guilt can make a person pun-ish themselves over and over and over again.

I'll take a conflict between strangers or natural enemies any day. A family tussle could last for years and never be resolved.

I made my plans to meet the women at the doctor's office, both to make sure they were OK and to begin the process of healing. It wasn't what I wanted, but it's what I do.

Surprisingly, I wasn't needed in the least. If I'd have written out all my worries and fears and checked off those that came true, I'd have to make a mark next to "None of the Above."

Oh, the injuries were real, very real. Bev was in some real pain and was looking at a long recovery. It was going to make it very difficult for her to do the things she enjoyed doing—especially golf. The doctor didn't want to predict when—if ever—she would be out on the links again, but he didn't sound hopeful. Bev's biggest concern at the moment, however, was how she'd be able to con-tinue to organize a charity tournament that was coming up, injury or not.

Bev didn't blame her sister in the least. The cart had taken off, and Anna in her panic had confused the pedals, making the injury worst. But Bev knew her sister hadn't planned her any harm.

As for Anna, she simply told me, "I know I had no inten-tion of hurting my sister. She knows that too." She felt bad, but not guilty. Maybe it's because I come from a big city where people are always either suing each other, or threatening to do so, that I was more than a little shocked. I was pleasantly surprised, but shocked nevertheless. We live in a world where nothing is an accident. Every inci-dent could become the cause of legal action—or at the very least a long-lasting grudge.

More than three years have gone by since the accident. The women have taken up golf again. And their relationship seems like a normal one for sisters—no more than the usual arguments, rolling eyes, and half smiles that say, "What do you expect, we're sisters?"

But there's been no resentment and not a word that I have ever heard of recrimination or regret. Why?

Three reasons, near as I can tell. First of all, both are women of faith. Their faith is at the center of their lives, and that is what's most important.

Second, they genuinely love each other. They're alike and different and you sometimes wonder how they can ever get along, much less live together, but love makes just about everything possible.

But I think the most important reason is because they are golfers.

Golfers know that life never works out the way you expect it. No matter how much you train, the unexpected is always lurking around the corner. You may defeat your partner, but you never beat the game of golf. There are always surprises—pleasant and unpleasant. So life is what you make of it.

And because you're pretty sure that nothing will ever work out exactly the way you'd like, but things will work out one way or another, you have hope. There's always hope that this day will be different. Whether out on the course or in life, something good may happen that puts all the bad things in perspective.

This is just a theory of mine. But it makes sense, at least to me.

Frank Ramirez

Riders

Playing golf isn't any fun if you're not having fun playing.

Joyce Wethered

Sandies, Barkies, Greenies . . . after a while you think you have heard all the golf terms. And just when you think you've heard it all, this wonderful game produces one more moment, one more word . . . that will tickle you for a lifetime.

It's a sun-filled morning at the local club. We are having a mixed scramble event in which we pick random partners from a hat. It's a nice way to meet and greet new people, and in four hours you do get to know a lot about the people you play with.

After the hat-picking, my all-star team consists of two young flat-bellies, one who can hit the ball a mile, and Mildred. Mildred is one of the matriarchs and charming legends of our club. She may be in her mideighties, but who is counting?

As we walk to our carts, Mildred takes my hand and

asks if it would be all right if her friend Helen joined our team: "We do so like to ride together."

"But Helen is on another team," I explain.

"I'm sure a bright young man like you will figure all that out," she smiles.

Who can say no to that pretty smile, a smile that belongs to one of the original founders of our club?

The player negotiations go well; after all, I'm trading a young gun/single-digit handicapper for Helen, also in her mideighties . . . I'm also getting a first-round draft choice for next year's mixed scramble.

I think I hear snickering as I turn and walk back to tell Mildred that her friend Helen is now part of our team.

The day goes as expected. Mildred and Helen struggle a wee bit from the tee, and their irons are not as crisp as they hoped. But the ladies putt well, and as you know, in a scramble putting is the name of the game. We have a fun-filled day, and I learn a lot more about the history of the course. Our young-gun partner has a great ball-striking day, so he's happy and the ladies are wonderful cheerleaders for our needy male egos.

We have almost reached a respectable score, and with some luck we might be in line to win a pair of socks or bag of tees. Our foursome is now circled anxiously around a patio table enjoying a pitcher of beer. And yes, Mildred and Helen are joining us in our beverage of choice. As we wait for the important announcement of the winning teams, Helen buys each of us a raffle ticket and handing them to us says, "I don't play so well anymore, but I still raffle well, so don't lose your ticket."

Mildred is gushing with compliments to our flat-bellied superstar of the day as Helen settles back into her chair.

"And you, Helen, you played wonderfully; did you have four Riders or five?" asks Mildred.

My male companion looks at me with "Huh?" written

all over his face. My shoulders shrug and we let it drop. He finishes his drink and raises his hand for the waitress. But I catch his look, his question. Then finally, not being able to hold it back any longer, he asks Mildred, "Did you say that Helen had four or five Riders? What's a Rider?"

"Oh, a Rider is when either Helen or I hit the ball far enough that we need to RIDE in the golf cart to reach our next shot," says Mildred finishing the last drop in her beer glass.

It's an amazing game we play; the excitement of your first par, breaking 100, 90, 80. . . . Watching your kids play. And someday I hope we all experience the joy of four or five "Riders" in one round.

The moments, the words, and the thrills just keep coming.

Bill Giering

Teaching Golf Is Life Touching!

The capacity to care is the thing that gives life its deepest meaning and significance.

Pablo Casals

It is 7 AM at Sweetwater Country Club. What a beautiful morning! It's already humid, but the sun is not yet scorching. As I head out to the range to set up my "office" for the day, I see that the maintenance staff has not finished mowing. I settle into my cart to wait as one of my coworkers approaches me, talking fluently in Spanish, while I listen and dissect his conversation with my limited bilingual training. He has a question about how to hold the club. I oblige and show him some possibilities for him to consider. I sense his appreciation immediately with his huge grin, and he helps me unload my cart of "stuff" and we go about our day. A few days later, I see him by the maintenance barn showing his son what I had shown him about holding the golf club. They both turn to give me a "thumbs-up" and make my day.

It's high noon at Sweetwater Country Club, ninety-five degrees today with 90 percent humidity. As I head toward my cart to go inside for a lunch break, I notice one of our senior golfers working on his game, in obvious disappointment. Our eyes meet and without a word being said, I sensed his frustration. *How can you not want to help a struggling senior golfer willing to work at his golf game in this kind of weather?* I visit with him a bit, and as he explains his challenge, it becomes obvious that he is not aiming and aligning well. We go over this in a simple explanation, and his grin after hitting one down the middle makes my day . . . suddenly I am not so tired after a busy morning of teaching. I head in for lunch with renewed energy for the afternoon. Later that week, I see him and his wife returning at dusk after playing nine holes, and he flags me down to share his success on the course that afternoon, again making my day.

It is 6:00 PM at Sweetwater Country Club. Our range is filled and my last lesson of the day is beginning. A married couple, new golfers, come for their first full-swing lesson. After introductions and some conversation, we begin my progression of learning to move with the club, learning to clip grass, learning to clip the tee, and finally, learning to clip the tee with the ball on top. The complete joy these two new golfers exhibit when that first golf ball goes into the air toward the target is priceless . . . you cannot imagine the expressions on their face when this happens. Days later, I see them practicing on the range and this scenario repeats itself. It makes my day.

It is 7:30 PM and I am reloading my cart of "stuff," heading back to the clubhouse. The sun is beginning to diminish and the weather is cooling a bit . . . a lovely time of night. One of my junior golfers is putting on the green near the clubhouse, by himself. I give a "shout-out" and sense something unusual when this usually boisterous, energetic golfer gives me only a small wave. I stop my cart and head over to chat. His performance in the tournament earlier today was "pathetic" (his words) due to his putting and would I mind watching him roll a few? As I watched, chatted, and teased (as I often do), I saw and understood that it was not a physical putting challenge . . . his mechanics were fine. Only after we talked did we both understand that his work schedule and his golf schedule were not in balance, and possible fatigue led to a loss of concentration and focus during the round. His apparent relief in hearing and believing this helped him roll a few beautiful putts, his confidence restored. He hops in my cart and we grab a Coke out of my office refrigerator while unloading my teaching "stuff." Then he heads for home with a smile on his face. It makes my day.

I head home with a smile on my face too—tired and sweaty, but inspired, enlightened, and filled with gratitude.

I call my mentor/teacher Betsy Cullen to discuss our teaching for the day, our usual routine. Sharing, laughing, learning, reflecting with this extraordinary teacher who has taught me so much made my day. Do I really have the energy to head to my Bikram yoga class after this long day in the sun and heat? You better believe it . . . it will help me help others tomorrow.

Debbie Vangellow

Reprinted by permission of Cartoon Resource and Marlies Killet. © 2006 Cartoon Resource and Marlies Killet.

More Chicken Soup?

Many of the stories and poems you have read in this book were submitted by readers like you who had read earlier Chicken Soup for the Soul books. We publish many Chicken Soup for the Soul books every year. We invite you to contribute a story to one of these future volumes.

Stories may be up to twelve hundred words and must uplift or inspire. You may submit an original piece, something you have read, or your favorite quotation on your refrigerator door.

To obtain a copy of our submission guidelines and a listing of upcoming Chicken Soup books, please write, fax, or check one of our websites.

Please send your submissions to:

Chicken Soup for the Soul
Website: www.chickensoup.com
P.O. Box 30880
Santa Barbara, CA 93130
fax: 805-563-2945

We will be sure that both you and the author are credited for your submission.

For information about speaking engagements, other books, audiotapes, workshops, and training programs, please contact any of our authors directly.

In Support of Others

In the spirit of supporting others, the publisher and coauthors of *Chicken Soup for the Woman Golfer's Soul* will donate a minimum of 2.5 cents per book to:

Y-ME National Breast Cancer Organization

Y-ME National Breast Cancer Organization (Y-ME) is a Chicago-based national nonprofit organization with the mission to ensure, through information, empowerment, and peer support, that no one faces breast cancer alone. Y-ME does not raise money for research. We're here today for those who can't wait for tomorrow's cure.

At the center of the organization is the Y-ME National Breast Cancer Hotline, the only 24/7 call center operated by trained peer counselors who are breast cancer survivors, and it takes more than 40,000 calls a year. Y-ME counselors do not give medical advice but give emotional support and information about breast cancer, procedures, and treatment options. Hotline calls are interpreted in 150 languages.

Y-ME's newsletters, publications, brochures, and website, www.y-me.org, provide information and support to those touched by breast cancer in Spanish and English. Other Y-ME programs include a Match Program for both patients who have similar diagnoses and life experiences, and for husbands and partners of women with breast cancer; the Wig & Prosthesis Bank for those with limited resources; the monthly ShareRing Network Teleconference; and *A Day for You* and *Friends of Ann & Mimi*, programs for the medically underserved.

Y-ME's Advocacy program works to increase breast cancer research funding, support breast cancer–related clinical study, and ensures quality health care for all.

The organization has affiliates throughout the nation

that provide services such as support groups, early detection and teen workshops, wigs and prostheses for women with limited resources, and advocacy on breast cancer related policies in their communities.

Each year on Mother's Day, the organization holds the Y-ME Race to Empower in Chicago and Y-ME Walk to Empower events across the country. In 2006, nearly 40,000 people took part, raising a total of $6 million in Chicago, Denver, Houston, Miami, Sacramento, San Diego, Seattle, Tulsa, and Washington, D.C. Eighty percent of each dollar raised benefits programs and services offered free of charge to those seeking information and support when facing breast cancer. Y-ME is further expanding its Mother's Day tradition by adding Walk to Empower events in Atlanta, Cleveland, and Phoenix in 2007.

Charity Navigator, an independent evaluator of nonprofits, gives Y-ME its highest rating of four stars for sound fiscal management. Y-ME meets all of the National Health Council's 41 Standards of Excellence, best practices that encompass the areas of governance, personnel policies, programs finance, fund-raising, accounting and reporting, and evaluation.

In 2006, Eaton Corporation's Golf Grip Division teamed up with Y-ME through the "Grip for Awareness, Swing for Hope" campaign helping to ensure that no one faces breast cancer alone. Eaton's Golf Grip Division donated $.25 to Y-ME from every one of its Golf Pride® Tour Velvet® Pink and Dual Durometer™ Pink putter grips sold in the USA, Japan, and the UK. This tradition will continue in 2007.

If you or someone you know needs breast cancer information or support, call the 24-hour Y-ME National Breast Cancer Hotline at 1-800-221-2141 or 1-800-986-9505 (Spanish).

Who Is Jack Canfield?

Jack Canfield is the cocreator and editor of the Chicken Soup for the Soul series, which *Time* magazine has called "the publishing phenomenon of the decade." The series now has 105 titles with over 100 million copies in print in forty-one languages. Jack is also the coauthor of eight other bestselling books including *The Success Principles: How to Get from Where You Are to Where You Want to Be, Dare to Win, The Aladdin Factor, You've Got to Read This Book,* and *The Power of Focus: How to Hit Your Business and Personal and Financial Targets with Absolute Certainty.*

Jack has recently developed a telephone coaching program and an online coaching program based on his most recent book *The Success Principles.* He also offers a seven-day Breakthrough to Success seminar every summer, which attracts 400 people from fifteen countries around the world.

Jack has conducted intensive personal and professional development seminars on the principles of success for over 900,000 people in twenty-one countries around the world. He has spoken to hundreds of thousands of others at numerous conferences and conventions and has been seen by millions of viewers on national television shows such as *The Today Show, Fox and Friends, Inside Edition, Hard Copy,* CNN's *Talk Back Live, 20/20, Eye to Eye,* the NBC *Nightly News,* and the CBS *Evening News.*

Jack is the recipient of many awards and honors, including three honorary doctorates and a Guinness World Records Certificate for having seven books from the Chicken Soup for the Soul series appearing on the *New York Times* bestseller list on May 24, 1998.

To write to Jack or for inquiries about Jack as a speaker, his coaching programs, or his seminars, use the following contact information:

The Canfield Companies
P.O. Box 30880 • Santa Barbara, CA 93130
phone: 805-563-2935 • fax: 805-563-2945
E-mail: info@jackcanfield.com or
visit his website at www.jackcanfield.com

Who Is Mark Victor Hansen?

In the area of human potential, no one is more respected than Mark Victor Hansen. For more than thirty years, Mark has focused solely on helping people from all walks of life reshape their personal vision of what's possible. His powerful messages of possibility, opportunity, and action have created powerful change in thousands of organizations and millions of individuals worldwide.

He is a sought-after keynote speaker, bestselling author, and marketing maven. Mark's credentials include a lifetime of entrepreneurial success and an extensive academic background. He is a prolific writer with many bestselling books, such as *The One Minute Millionaire, Cracking the Millionaire Code, How to Make the Rest of Your Life the Best of Your Life, The Power of Focus, The Aladdin Factor,* and *Dare to Win,* in addition to the Chicken Soup for the Soul series. Mark has made a profound influence through his library of audios, videos, and articles in the areas of big thinking, sales achievement, wealth building, publishing success, and personal and professional development.

Mark is the founder of the MEGA Seminar Series. MEGA Book Marketing University and Building Your MEGA Speaking Empire are annual conferences where Mark coaches and teaches new and aspiring authors, speakers, and experts on building lucrative publishing and speaking careers. Other MEGA events include MEGA Info-Marketing and My MEGA Life.

As a philanthropist and humanitarian, Mark works tirelessly for organizations such as Habitat for Humanity, American Red Cross, March of Dimes, Childhelp USA, and many others. He is the recipient of numerous awards that honor his entrepreneurial spirit, philanthropic heart, and business acumen. He is a lifetime member of the Horatio Alger Association of Distinguished Americans, an organization that honored Mark with the prestigious Horatio Alger Award for his extraordinary life achievements.

Mark Victor Hansen is an enthusiastic crusader of what's possible and is driven to make the world a better place.

Mark Victor Hansen & Associates, Inc.
P.O. Box 7665 • Newport Beach, CA 92658
phone: 949-764-2640 • fax: 949-722-6912
www.markvictorhansen.com

Who Is Matthew E. Adams?

Matthew E. Adams is a twenty-year veteran of the golf industry in addition to being a *New York Times* and *USA Today* bestselling author, professional speaker, and entrepreneur, who is committed to improving the lives of others.

Matthew has coauthored many Chicken Soup for the Soul books, including *Chicken Soup for the Soul of America* and *Chicken Soup for the NASCAR Soul* in addition to contributing to numerous Chicken Soup for the Soul projects. In 2006, Matthew authored *Fairways of Life— Wisdom and Inspiration from the Greatest Game*. Matthew began his career at ESPN and can be seen regularly on the Golf Channel.

Matthew's work has been featured in publications all over the globe, including the *Los Angeles Times*.

Matthew is a dynamic and highly sought after speaker. If you wish to contact Matthew or schedule him for your next event, his office can be reached at www.FairwaysofLife.com, or for speaking engagements visit www.GolfPodium.com.

Who Is Patty Aubery?

As the president of Chicken Soup for the Soul Enterprises and a #1 *New York Times* bestselling coauthor, Patty Aubery knows what it's like to juggle work, family and social obligations—along with the responsibility of developing and marketing the more than 80 million *Chicken Soup* books and licensed goods worldwide.

She knows because she's been with Jack Canfield's organization since the early days—before *Chicken Soup* took the country by storm. Jack was still telling these heartwarming stories then, in his training programs, workshops and keynote presentations, and it was Patty who directed the labor of love that went into compiling and editing the original 101 *Chicken Soup* stories. Later, she supported the daunting marketing effort and steadfast optimism required to bring it to millions of readers worldwide.

Today, Patty is the mother of two active boys—J. T. and Chandler—exemplifying that special combination of commitment, organization and life balance all working women want to have.

Of her part in the *Chicken Soup* family, Patty says, "I'm always encouraged, amazed and humbled by the storytellers I meet when working on any *Chicken Soup* book, but by far the most poignant have been those stories of women in the working world, overcoming incredible odds and—in the face of all challenges—excelling as only women could do."

Patty is also the coauthor of several other bestselling titles: *Chicken Soup for the Christian Soul, Christian Family Soul* and *Christian Woman's Soul, Chicken Soup for the Expectant Mother's Soul, Chicken Soup for the Sister's Soul* and *Chicken Soup for the Surviving Soul.*

Together Patty and husband, Jeff, have been committed to golf as a lifetime passion and have traveled the world extensively in pursuit of the game and the industry that surrounds it. They are most proud of Jeff's tireless work to help bring millions of people to the game of golf by developing programs and products that are accessible and affordable for everyone.

Together with J. T. and Chandler, Patty and Jeff make their home in Santa Barbara, California. Patty can be reached at:

Self-Esteem Seminars
P.O. Box 30880
Santa Barbara, CA 93130
Phone: 805-563-2935
Fax: 805-563-2945

Contributors

Donna Adams received her bachelor of science in finance from the University of Florida in 1989. She is a choreographer and singer for the Coastline Show Chorus, currently a fourth-place international medalist. She also sings tenor in an a *cappella* quartet. She currently lives in North Kingstown, Rhode Island, with her husband and two sons.

Aaron Bacall has graduate degrees in organic chemistry as well as in educational administration and supervision from New York University. He has been a pharmaceutical research chemist, teacher, and cartoonist. He has sold his cartoons to most national publications and has had seven books of his cartoons published. Three of his cartoons are featured in the permanent collection at the Harvard Business School's Baker Library. He continues to create and sell his cartoons and is writing a script for a stage play as well.

Suzanne A. Baginskie recently retired from her job as a law office manager/paralegal, which she held for more than twenty-five years. She has been published in other Chicken Soup for the Soul books, *Cats Magazine, True Romance,* and several nonfiction articles. She lives on the west coast of Florida with her husband, Al.

Kathryn Beisner is a writer and motivational storyteller. Her love of history and family traditions is celebrated in her popular audio book *Ordinary Women with Extraordinary Spirit!* and by essay in "Olé! Posole!" Kathryn lives by the motto "No Guts, No Story!" For more adventures visit www.kbsproductions.com.

Susie Maxwell Berning, professional golfer for forty years, winner of thirteen LPGA tournaments, four of which were majors, three U.S. Opens and the Western Open. She is the mother of two daughters, Robing and Cindy. Robing and her mom were the first mother and daughter to compete in an LPGA event together. Robing played on the Ohio Women's golf team; Cindy has a great swing but plays very little. Susie teaches golf in the winter at the reserve golf club in Indian Well and in the summer at Maroon Creek Golf Club.

Heather Black is a writer living in Gainsville, Florida.

Jane Blalock is the winner of twenty-seven Ladies Professional Golf Association (LPGA) tournaments, commissioner of the LPGA Legends Tour, president/CEO of JBCGolf, Inc., and founder of the LPGA Golf Clinics for Women.

Martha Campbell is a graduate of Washington University, St. Louis School of Fine Arts, and a former writer/designer for Hallmark Cards. She has been a freelance cartoonist and book illustrator since 1973. She can be reached at P.O. Box 2538, Harrison, AR, or at marthaf@alltel.net.

Helen Casey is a member of the International Network of Golf, Golf Writers Association of America (GWAA), and is one of the founders of Women in the Golf Industry (WIGI). When it comes to golf, Helen says she would rather talk a good game than play one! Helen Casey resides in Naples, Florida, with her husband Sam. She may be reached at info@augustagolfstories.com.

Helen C. Colella is a freelance writer from Colorado. She has published educational books, as well as fiction and nonfiction articles and stories for adults and children. Her work has been published in other Chicken Soup for the Soul books and in parenting/general interest magazines. She operates AssitWrite as a consultant for self-publishers.

Lisa Conley is a Class-A Member of the LPGA T&CP, married to Steve Conley, PGA Member. Parents Ken and Doris Earls introduced Lisa to golf at the ripe old age of five. Lisa's hobbies include writing, golf, travel, movies, and being with close friends and family.

Heather Cook is a writer and mother in Calgary, Alberta. She writes non-fiction articles and currently has a horse-related nonfiction book under consideration for publication in 2007. She enjoys reading, horseback riding, and low-pressure mini golf. Please e-mail her at hlcook@shaw.ca.

Diana D'Alessio received her bachelor of arts from Furman University in 1997. She has been a member of the LPGA Tour's Tournament Division for the past seven years. Diana enjoys cooking, mountain biking, tennis, movies, fishing, and barbecuing with her five brothers. Please e-mail her at DDAlessio69@aol.com.

Barbara Davey is a vice president at Christ Hospital in Jersey City, New Jersey, where she is responsible for marketing, public relations, and fund-raising. She is a graduate of Seton Hall University, where she received her bachelor's and master's degrees. She and her husband, Reinhold Becker, live in Verona, New Jersey. She may be reached at wisewords2@aol.com.

Diana Fairbanks DeMeo received her bachelor's in psychology from University of California, San Diego, giving her just enough knowledge to be dangerous. When not writing about her favorite subject—human quirks and foibles—Diana can be found working in information technology sales and playing in the ocean or the great outdoors.

Terri K. Duncan received her bachelor's, master's, and specialist degrees from Augusta State University. She is currently pursuing her doctoral degree at Georgia Southern University and is also a graduation specialist at Greenbrier High School. Terri enjoys spending time with her husband and two teenagers. Writing is her therapy.

Katharine Dyson is a golf and travel writer for several national publications, as well as a guidebook author. Her golf journeys have taken her to Africa, Argentina, Canada, Britain, France, Portugal, and other places. She is a member of the Golf Writers Association of America and Society of American Travel Writers. She lives in Ridgefield, Connecticut.

Carolyn Ford grew up on Staten Island in New York City and now lives on the Jersey shore. She writes stories for young readers, as well as essays and poetry. She meets with a wonderful writing group every week and volunteers in a grade-school reading program.

Mary Murphy Fox received her bachelor of arts and master of science degrees from Marywood University. She is a supervisor of special education in Pennsylvania. She enjoys gardening, writing, and golfing. She resides in the Endless Mountains with her husband, Steve, and their dog, Fuzzy. Please e-mail her at foxmm2004@yahoo.com.

William Giering is a New York–based writer who writes and speaks about business and golf. His work has appeared in major national magazines and newspapers. He has played golf on every continent and covered all four majors . . . and he still can't putt.

Joanie Gilmore is retired from an executive assistant/public relations career of twenty-five years. She is the author or *North Whidbey Pioneer Schools* and has also published short stories for the Chicken Soup for the Soul series and other publications. Joan loves writing and working in orphanages on the Baja, Mexico.

Anne Marie Goslak is an LPGA teaching professional in Winston-Salem, North Carolina. She has been teaching in the area for more than sixteen years. Anne Marie loves to compete and dreams of playing in the U.S. Open one day. She can be reached at www.golfwithannemarie.com

Natalie Gulbis started playing golf at the age of four. At the age of fourteen, Gulbis won the California Women's Amateur Championship and is one of the LPGA's fastest-rising stars ranking 14th on the LPGA money list. Her hobbies include working out and running.

Maria Harden was inspired by an eighth-grade teacher, who encouraged her to pursue her interest in writing. This was the impetus that generated her lifelong love affair with the wily word. She is widely published on the Internet, as well as in newspapers, magazines, and anthologies. E-mail Maria at mharden@mts.net.

Jamie Hullett is a graduate of Texas A&M University. She played golf for the Aggies from 1994 to 1998. Jamie has been a professional golfer since 1999, competing in her seventh season on the LPGA tour.

Clinical psychologist **Roberta Isleib** took up writing to justify time spent on the links. Her golf mysteries, including *Six Strokes Under* and *Putt to Death*, were nominated for both Agatha and Anthony awards. *Deadly Advice*, the first of a mystery series starring a Connecticut psychologist/advice columnist, debuts in 2007.

Marilyn Jaskulke, grandmother of eleven and great-grandmother of three, enjoys time with her families in Minnesota and California. She writes, plays golf, and sews quilts for her churches' mission projects. Please e-mail her at mar68jask@cox.net.

Marlies Killat was born in 1967 near Hamburg, North Germany. He began creating cartoons in December 2002. Two years ago, he quit his job and now lives as an artist in Frankfurt am Main, Germany. Postcards with Killat's cartoons are widely available in German shops. His cartoons also appear in Germany's well-known magazines such as *FOCUS Money* and *Handelsblatt*.

Betty King is author of several publications, including *It Takes Two Mountains to Make a Valley, But—It was in the Valleys I Grew*, and *The Fragrance of Life*. She is a lifestyle and devotional newspaper columnist. She lives with the disease multiple sclerosis. Learn more at www.bettyking.net or contact her at baking2@charter.net.

Joe Kohl has been a cartoonist and illustrator since 1972. His work has appeared in many major magazines. He has also illustrated numerous greeting cards, T-shirts, and mugs, as well as books and advertising illustrations. His website is http://joekohl.com.

Tom Krause is an international speaker, author, and poet. He currently lives in Nixa, Missouri, with wife, Amy, and sons, Tyler and Sam. Contact him at www.coachkrause.com.

Nancy Lewis has been a member of the LPGA since 1990. She holds a bachelor of arts in public relations and master of arts in higher education administration from San Jose State University, where she played golf collegiately. She and her husband, Dave, own Stripes Practice Center in Tracy, California.

Jennifer Martin is an educator, TV producer/hostess, and author of *The Huna Warrior: The Magic Begins*. She loves writing stories for Chicken Soup for the Soul books, lives in northern California, and can be reached at jenmartin@ hunawarrior.com. Please visit her website at www.hunawarrior.com.

Upon retiring from the LPGA Tour, **Terry-Jo Myers** accepted a gubernatorial appointment to sit on the board of directors for the Florida Sports Foundation, as well as continuing her efforts with Ortho-McNeil to educate the consumer and physician on interstitial cystitis. Please email her at tjiclpga@comcast.net.

Rachel S. Neal aced a hole once. Unfortunately her drive from the seventh tee box fell into the fifth-hole cup, thanks to the rock that she nailed. She writes to promote laughter, faith, and spiritual growth. She enjoys life wth her husband and cats in Montana.

Ann O'Farrell has a master of arts from Trinity College, Dublin, where she subsequently tutored as a drama therapist. Now retired to Florida with her husband, she is forging a second career as a writer. Ann has also written *Norah's Children*, a historical novel set in rural Ireland. Please e-mail her at annofarrell@aol.com.

A native of Tennessee, **Cary Osborne** has lived in several states and for a short time in France. She currently lives in Oklahoma. Never tiring of learning, she is pursuing a master's degree in library and information studies at the University of Oklahoma. She can be reached by e-mail at iroshi@cox.net.

Celeste T. Palermo lives in Colorado with her husband, Pete, and daughters Peyton and Morgan. She writes a column for the *Parker Chronicle*, is a contributor to *Broncos Magazine*, and has an inspirational website, www.thegirlsletter.com. She is the author of *From the Red Tees* (Cumberland House, 2007). Please contact her at coceleste@aol.com.

Joan Paquette is a freelance and children's writer who lives near Boston, Massachusetts.

Kristal Parker-Manzo has been an active LPGA tour member since 1995 and a touring golf professional since 1987. She is married with two children and lives in Phoenix, Arizona. Her priorities are her family and church. Her hobbies include all sports, music, reading, and great shared laughs with her friends.

Frank Ramirez has served as a pastor in the Church of the Brethren in California, Indiana, and Pennsylvania. He and his wife, Jennie, share three adult children, Francisco, Jessica, and Jacob, and three grandchildren. Frank has published over thirty books, including *The Meanest Man in Patrick County* (Brethren Press).

Pat Hentz Regensburg has a book of poetry out, *Backward Glances at a Triumphantly Neurotic Life*. If you read this story, you will understand where the book came from. She lives in Florida and Maine with her husband and three not-too-well-behaved, but charming, dogs. You can e-mail her at aregens@aol.com.

Angie Rizzo graduated from the University of Oregon in 2000 with a bachelor's degree in business and sports marketing. Angie is currently playing on the LPGA Tour and also enjoys spending time with her family and friends, scrapbooking, and traveling.

Sallie A. Rodman lives in Los Alamitos, California, with her husband, cat, and a dog. Her work has appeared in *Chicken Soup for the Soul* anthologies, the *Orange County Register*, and various magazines. She loves writing inspirational pieces and is currently working on her memoir, *Panic Demons; My Life with Panic Attacks and Agoraphobia*. Write her at sa.rodman@verizon.net.

Kristen Samp recieved bachelor of arts degrees in English and philosophy from the University of Missouri, where she competed on the women's golf team. She has been a touring golf professional since 1997. Kristen enjoys biking, reading, running, and spending time with family.

Mike Shapiro's cartoons appear in many publications, including the *Wall Street Journal, Barron's, The Harvard Business Review,* and *Reader's Digest.* He is also a contributor to many legal, medical, and business journals and has done work for animation studios as well as advertising agencies. In addition to the above, Mike frequently draws caricatures at live events. Mike lives in Washington, D.C., with his wife, Amy, their son, Jacob, and two noisy dogs.

Patty Sheehan is fifty years old and an LPGA Hall of Fame member and World Golf Hall of Fame member. She has two children, ages seven and nine. Her hobbies are gardening, helping at the kids' schools, and most importantly, raising her two wonderful children. Patty still plays tournaments both on the LPGA and the Legends Tour (Women's Senior Tour).

Ann Sheridan is the founder of Bimbo's Buddies (www.bimbosbuddies.org), and will soon publish *Dogs Get Cancer Too,* a picture book in which her pet dog Bimbo offers hope and encouragement to children battling cancer. Ann is a breast cancer survivor. She resides in Long Branch, New Jersey.

Christine Smith is fifty-six, married thirty-eight years, has three children, thirteen grandchildren, and many foster children. Her stories have been published in two previous Chicken Soup for the Soul books, *Woman's World, Heartwarmers,* and monthly in a foster care newsletter. Her passions are children, writing, and serving God. E-mail her at iluvmyfamilyxxx000@yahoo.com.

LPGA cofounder and three-time LPGA president **Marilynn Smith** is recognized as one of golf's greatest ambassadors. She visited all fifty states and thirty-six countries promoting, organizing, and playing golf. Winner of twenty LPGA tournaments, including two majors such as the Titleholders in 2006 Marilynn was inducted into the World Golf Hall of Fame.

Stacy Smith is a freelance writer who thrives on writing about cultural and spiritual experiences while traveling. Between her journeys and quests for inspiration, she pays the bills by writing copy for businesses and planning meetings and events. You can contact her through her website at www.wordsmith-writing.com, or at wordsmith.writing@earthlink.net.

Marcia Swearingen is a former newspaper editor and columnist, now freelancing full-time. She serves on the local board of Bethany Christian Services and facilitates a group of Christian writers. She and her husband, Jim, are the parents of a grown daughter. Her e-mail address is mswearingen@comcast.net.

Perry Swenson graduated from the University of Texas, where she competed on the nationally ranked women's golf team and earned a degree in finance in 2005. She currently plays on the professional tour and also enjoys traveling, singing, playing the piano, mountain biking, and working out. Please e-mail her at Perry_Swenson@hotmail.com.

B. J. Taylor is a *Guideposts* special correspondent/writer and has been published in numerous magazines, newspapers, and many Chicken Soup for the Soul books. She loves playing golf with her girlfriends almost every week. B.J. has a golfing husband (with a much lower handicap), two sons, and two adorable grandsons. You can reach B.J. through her website at www.clik.to/bjtaylor.

Tana Figueras Thomas is an LPGA teaching professional in suburban Philadelphia. She is a former Division I golf coach and a member of the Arizona State University Golf Team (1988/1992) and NCAA Champions 1990. She earned a bachelor of arts in humanities in 1992. Tana enjoys all sports, teaching, coaching, movies, and travel.

She is the mother of two young boys, Anthony and Glenallen, and wife of Glen Thomas. She hopes to one day return to her coaching career.

Deb Vangellow holds both bachelor of arts and master of science degrees from the University of Northern Iowa and Miami (Ohio) University, respectively. She is the director of instruction at Sweetwater Country Club in Houston, Texas, and is on the renowned faculty for the LPGA National Education Program. Please e-mail her at debbievang@earthlink.net.

Karen Weiss is a graduate of the University of Minnesota and a thirteen-year member of the LPGA Tour. She is retiring in 2006 to pursue a master's degree in horticulture and lives in St. Paul, Minnesota.

Ashanti L. White received her bachelor of arts in political science and African American Studies in 2003. A writer for *DV8 Magazine*, her works have also appeared in the *Corradi* and *Eternal Portraits*. In addition to performing professionlly, she is currently writing her first novel. Please e-mail her at alwdct@yahoo.com.

Kathy Ann Whitworth, an LPGA Hall of Fame member, played the LPGA Tour for thirty-one years. She holds the record of eighty-eight official tournament wins, more than any LPGA or PGA player. Now retired, she makes personal appearances for charity events and does some teaching.

Ann Wolta is an LPGA Class "A" Teaching Professional in Arvada, Colorado. She has been teaching golf for twenty-four years and earned many outstanding teacher awards. Ann enjoys teaching and playing golf, dancing, and traveling. Please e-mail her at dancingfeather7@aol.com.

Woody Woodburn lives in Ventura, California, and is a member of the Jim Murray Memorial Foundation's Journalists Hall of Fame. He can be contacted at woodywoodburn99@aol.com.

Pamela M. Woods is the oldest of seven siblings. She graduated in 1965 and married her high school sweetheart in 1966. She has two beautiful daughters and five wonderful grandchildren. She started playing golf at age fifty. Some say she's addicted to the game. Is playing six days a week addicting? NO WAY!

Helen Xenakis is enjoying her retirement on Hilton Head Island, swimming, biking, golfing, and of course, writing. This is her second Chicken Soup for the Soul publication, and she looks forward to many more.

Thousands of **Bob Zahn**'s cartoons have been published in all the leading publications. He has more than one thousand greeting cards to his credit, as well as several humor books. His e-mail address is zahntoons@aol.com. Visit his website at www.zahntoons.com.